The First Era of Islamic Leadership

Unity to Civil War

Islamic Time line 632-661

Dr. Shaikh Mohammad Shahriyar Wahab

Copyright Notice

© 2025 Dr. Shaikh Mohammad Shahriyar Wahab

All rights reserved.

No part of this book may be reproduced, stored in a retrieval system, transmitted, or distributed in any form or by any means — electronic, mechanical, photocopying, recording, or otherwise — without the prior written permission of the copyright holder, Dr. Shaikh Mohammad Shahriyar Wahab.Legal action may be taken for any unauthorised use, reproduction, or distribution of this book or any part thereof.

Legal Notice

This book is an original work by Dr. Shaikh Mohammad Shahriyar Wahab. All rights are exclusively reserved by the author.

No content from this publication, whether in part or whole, including any text, graphics, illustrations, or referenced material, may be copied, adapted, published, or used in any manner without obtaining formal permission in writing from the author.

Photo

Adobe

Disclaimer

This book represents the views, opinions, and understanding of Dr. Shaikh Mohammad Shahriyar Wahab, developed through his personal research, study, and reflections.

This book is not intended to serve as an official religious reference, scholarly authority, or final verdict on any religious matter or personality. It is a collection of thoughts and analysis based on the author's personal comprehension of the topics discussed.

Readers are strongly encouraged to exercise their own judgment, consult other qualified scholars, and form their own understanding — especially on sensitive matters concerning religion, faith, and personalities mentioned within this work.

Neither the author nor the publisher shall be held responsible for any interpretation, application, or

Dr. Shaikh Mohammad Shahriyar Wahab

consequences arising from the use of the material in this book.

Dedication

To my beloved mother, Syeda Quamrun Naher, who, by the mercy of Allah, has reached the blessed age of 80 in the year 2025.

Her unwavering prayers, boundless love, and quiet strength have been the cornerstone of my life's journey.

She is my greatest blessing in this world.

May Allah grant her continued health, peace, and the highest place in Jannah.

To the memory of all those who dedicated their lives to the pursuit of knowledge and understanding of the early Islamic world, particularly those scholars whose tireless research and insightful interpretations have illuminated this pivotal era.

This work is a testament to their intellectual contributions and a humble attempt to build upon their legacy.

It is also dedicated to history students, the future scholars who will continue to explore and interpret the complexities of the past, ensuring that the lessons learned from the Rashidun Caliphate remain relevant and insightful for future generations.

May this book serve as a small contribution to their ongoing intellectual endeavours and inspire a deeper understanding of the formative period of Islamic civilisation. Finally, this work is dedicated to the enduring spirit of inquiry and the unwavering commitment to truth-seeking at the heart of all historical scholarship.

Contents

Disclaimer	1
Dedication	3
Preface	11
Introduction	13
1. The Dawn of the Rashidun Caliphate: The Legacy of Muhammad(PBUH) and the Election of Abu Bakr(RA)	15
The Prophet Muhammad(PBUH)'s Death and the Succession Crisis	17
Abu Bakr(RA)s Consolidation of Power The Ridda Wars	23
Administrative and Legal Reforms under Abu Bakr(RA)	29
Economic Policies and Expansion Under Abu Bakr(RA)	35
Legacy of Abu Bakr(RA) and the Transition to Umar(RA)	41
2. Umar(RA) ibn al-Khattab: Consolidation and Expansion of the Caliphate	48
Umar's(RA)'s Administrative Reforms and Centralized Governance	49
Military Conquests During Umar(RA)'s Reign	55
Economic Policies and Infrastructure Development Under Umar(RA)	61
Legal and Judicial Systems under Umar(RA)	69
The Legacy of Umar(RA) and the Transition to Uthman(RA)	75
Chapter 3: Uthman(RA) ibn Affan: Challenges and Controversies	81
Uthman(RA)'s Early Reign and Administrative Challenges	83
Economic Policies and Accusations of Favoritism	89

	The Growing Opposition and the Seeds of the First Fitna	95
	The Assassination of Uthman(RA) and its Immediate Aftermath	101
	The Legacy of Uthman(RA) and the Transition to Ali(RA)	107
3.	Ali(RA) ibn Abi Talib: Leadership and the First Fitna	113
	Ali(RA)'s Accession and the Challenges of Leadership	115
	The Battle of Siffin and its Aftermath	121
	The Kharijites and the Challenges toAlis Authority	127
	The Battle of Nahrawan and the Suppression of the Kharijites	133
	The Assassination of Ali(RA) and the End of the Rashidun Caliphate	139
4.	The First Fitna: A Civil War that Shattered the Unity of the Caliphate	144
	The Causes of the First Fitna A Deep Dive into Political and Religious Divisions	145
	The Key Players in the First Fitna Ali(RA) Muawiya and their Supporters	151
	Military Campaigns and Battles of the First Fitna	157
	The Impact of the First Fitna on the Political and Religious Landscape of the Islamic World	163
	The Aftermath of the First Fitna A New Era in Islamic History	169
5.	The Legacy of the Rashidun Caliphate: A Foundation for Islamic Governance and its Lasting Influence	175

The Administrative and Legal Innovations of the Rashidun Caliphate	177
The Expansion and Consolidation of Islamic Rule	183
The Development of Islamic Law and Jurisprudence during the Rashidun Era	189
The Social and Cultural Impacts of the Rashidun Caliphate	195
The Enduring Legacy Lessons from the Rashidun Caliphate for Modern Governance	201
Acknowledgments	207
Glossary	209
About Author	211

Preface

This book explores the Rashidun Caliphate (632-661 CE), a period of profound transformation and significant challenges in early Islamic history. The four Rightly Guided Caliphs—Abu Bakr(RA), Umar(RA), Uthman(RA), and Ali(RA)—each left an indelible mark on the fledgling empire, shaping its political structures, legal systems, and military strategies. Their reigns, however, were not without considerable internal strife, culminating in the devastating First Fitna, a civil war that irrevocably altered the course of Islamic history.

This study aims to provide a balanced and insightful examination of this critical era, drawing upon a wide range of primary and secondary sources to reconstruct the time's political, social, and military realities.

The narrative strives to move beyond simplistic narratives, acknowledging the complexities and contradictions inherent in the period. While focusing on significant events and key figures, the analysis incorporates the perspectives of diverse groups and examines the various interpretations of historical events. By carefully analysing the decisions made by the four caliphs and the impact of those decisions on the broader Islamic world, we aim to provide the reader with a nuanced understanding of the foundations of early Islamic governance and its lasting legacy.

This book is intended for a broad audience, from academic researchers to students and history enthusiasts seeking a deeper understanding of this formative period.

Introduction

The Rashidun Caliphate, spanning a mere three decades, represents a crucial juncture in the history of Islam and the Middle East. Its legacy extends far beyond its relatively short duration, profoundly influencing the development of Islamic political thought, law, and culture. This period witnessed the remarkable expansion of the newly established Muslim community from the Arabian Peninsula to encompass vast swathes of the former Byzantine and Sasanian empires. This rapid expansion, however, was accompanied by internal challenges that tested the unity and stability of the burgeoning Caliphate.

The succession crises, the Ridda Wars, and the First Fitna contributed to the era's complexities. This book delves into these complexities, providing a detailed account of the reigns of each of the four caliphs.

We examine their leadership styles, administrative reforms, and military strategies, analysing their successes and failures. Each caliph faced unique challenges and made distinctive contributions to shaping the early Islamic state.

Abu Bakr(RA) consolidated power after the death of the Prophet Muhammad(PBUH), while Umar(RA) established a centralised administrative system and oversaw further military conquests. Uthman(RA)'s reign was marked by increasing political dissent, ultimately culminating in his assassination. Ali(RA)'s leadership was challenged by internal conflicts that led to the devastating First Fitna, a civil war that shattered the fragile unity of the Caliphate.

This book will also explore the social and economic structures of the time, illustrating the intricate relationships between different segments of the population and the challenges of governing such a rapidly expanding and diverse empire.

The analysis of the Rashidun Caliphate is not simply a historical exercise; it offers valuable insights into fundamental questions of leadership, governance, and the challenges of building and sustaining a multi-ethnic and multi-religious state.

The lessons learned from this pivotal era remain profoundly relevant to our understanding of political power, social cohesion, and the lasting legacy of historical events.

Chapter 1
The Dawn of the Rashidun Caliphate: The Legacy of Muhammad(PBUH) and the Election of Abu Bakr(RA)

The Prophet Muhammad(PBUH)'s Death and the Succession Crisis

The death of the Prophet Muhammad(PBUH) in 632 CE cast a profound shadow over the burgeoning Muslim community. The charismatic leader, who had unified disparate tribes and laid the foundations of a new faith, was gone. The ensuing vacuum created a period of profound uncertainty and anxiety, a crucible in which the future trajectory of Islam would be forged. The question of succession, seemingly simple on its face, ignited a complex web of political maneuvering, tribal loyalties, and competing interpretations of religious authority. The absence of a clearly defined mechanism for choosing a successor to the Prophet, a critical oversight in Medina's rapidly evolving political landscape, fueled intense debate and heightened tensions among the various factions within the community.

Medina, the heart of the nascent Muslim state, was a melting pot of diverse tribes – the Aws, the Khazraj, and the

Muhajirun (immigrants from Mecca), each with its power structure and vested interests. The sudden death of Muhammad(PBUH) triggered deep-seated anxieties within these groups. The fear of reverting to the pre-Islamic tribal rivalries and power struggles was palpable. The unifying force of the Prophet's charismatic leadership was gone, leaving a power vacuum threatening to unravel the fragile unity painstakingly achieved during his lifetime. The fragile peace, built upon the foundation of a shared faith, now hung precariously in the balance.

A palpable sense of loss and grief marked the immediate aftermath of the Prophet's death. The community, accustomed to his unwavering guidance, grappled with the immense challenge of selecting a successor who could command the respect and authority necessary to lead the nascent ummah (community). The absence of explicit instructions from the Prophet regarding succession compounded the difficulty, leaving room for diverse interpretations and competing claims.

Several prominent figures emerged as potential candidates for the caliphate, each possessing unique strengths and weaknesses and attracting the support of distinct factions within the community. Abu Bakr(RA), a close companion of the Prophet and his father-in-law, was a strong contender, respected for his piety, wisdom, and unwavering loyalty. Umar(RA) ibn al-Khattab, known for his firmness and decisiveness, was another influential figure, though his assertive nature potentially alienated some within the community. Ali(RA) ibn Abi Talib, the Prophet's cousin and son-in-law, held significant religious and familial authority.

Still, his quieter nature initially made him less prominent in the immediate power struggle. The lack of a clear consensus on the succession process fueled rivalries and exacerbated existing tensions. Negotiations were complex, with competing claims and allegiances.

The events surrounding Abu Bakr(RA)'s election are ambiguous, as different sources provide varying accounts. However, it is generally accepted that a series of meetings and discussions took place in the mosque of Medina, where prominent community figures deliberated on the crucial matter of succession. The discussions were undoubtedly intense and fraught with emotion, given the immense significance of the decision. While primary sources often lack precise details on the exact voting process or the number of participants, the overarching narrative points to a gradual consensus-building process, with Abu Bakr(RA) emerging as the most suitable candidate. His piety, close association with the Prophet, and demonstrable leadership qualities won over a significant portion of the community, paving the way for his eventual acceptance as the first caliph.

The arguments advanced in favour of Abu Bakr(RA) often emphasised his impeccable character, his unwavering devotion to Islam, and his close relationship with the Prophet. His supporters viewed him as the most fitting individual to maintain the nascent faith's integrity and uphold Muhammad(PBUH)'s legacy. Conversely, those who opposed his nomination often raised concerns about his lack of military prowess and his potential inability to lead the community during times of potential conflict effectively.

The arguments against Abu Bakr(RA)'s leadership stemmed from differing interpretations of religious authority. This debate would continue to shape the political landscape of the early Islamic world for generations to come.

The election of Abu Bakr(RA) was not without its dissenters. Ali(RA) ibn Abi Talib and a segment of the community initially hesitated to support Abu Bakr(RA)'s ascension fully. This initial reluctance, rooted in differing viewpoints on the ideal successor and the process itself, stemmed from complex issues of familial ties, loyalty, and interpretation of religious authority. The ensuing tensions highlighted the challenge of maintaining unity in the face of diverging opinions on matters of profound religious and political importance. However, even with these dissenting voices, Abu Bakr(RA)'s authority eventually solidified, primarily due to his adept political skills and willingness to negotiate with and address the concerns of those who opposed his leadership. The period immediately following Abu Bakr(RA)'s election laid the foundation for the evolving governance structure of the nascent Caliphate.

The anxieties of the various tribal groups were significant. The fear that the death of Muhammad(PBUH) might trigger a return to tribal warfare was very real. The community had to grapple not only with its grief over the Prophet's death but also with the looming spectre of internal strife. The stability of the newly formed community was at stake. The freshly established leadership had to navigate complex inter-tribal relations, maintain social harmony, and prevent the resurgence of pre-Islamic conflicts. The very survival of the nascent state depended upon its ability to avoid the disintegration into fragmented and warring tribal entities.

The period immediately following the Prophet's death was a pivotal moment in early Islamic history. The success or failure of the new leadership in navigating the complex political and social landscape would determine whether the Muslim community would prosper and grow or succumb to internal conflicts and external threats. The delicate balance between consolidating power and maintaining unity became the defining challenge of the early Caliphate, a challenge that Abu Bakr(RA) would immediately have to face with his elevation to the position of the first Caliph. The path ahead was precarious, fraught with danger and uncertainty, demanding skilful leadership and a profound commitment to the principles of the new faith.

Abu Bakr(RA)s Consolidation of Power The Ridda Wars

The death of the Prophet Muhammad(PBUH), while mourned deeply, also unleashed a potent wave of instability across the Arabian Peninsula. The unifying force of his personality and prophetic authority had held together a diverse collection of tribes, some recently converted to Islam, others still clinging to their ancestral beliefs. With his passing, the fragile unity began to unravel. Numerous tribes, particularly those on the periphery of the newly established Muslim community, saw an opportunity to reclaim their independence, casting off the allegiance sworn to Muhammad(PBUH). This wave of defections, fueled by a complex mix of factors including tribal rivalries, religious doubts, and opportunistic leadership, became known as the Ridda Wars, or Wars of Apostasy.

The immediate reaction within Medina was one of grave concern. The nascent Muslim state, barely established, found itself facing a potentially existential threat. The prospect of a fragmented Arabia, reverting to the pre-Islamic era of warring tribes, loomed large. Abu Bakr(RA), newly elected as Caliph, was thrust into the unenviable position of consolidating the freshly formed state whilst simultaneously suppressing a rebellion that threatened to dismantle it entirely. The challenge before him was monumental; to quell the widespread uprisings required both military strength and astute political strategy. The fledgling Caliphate possessed neither in abundance.

The scale of the rebellion was considerable. Tribes in Yemen, Najd, and other regions openly renounced their allegiance to Islam, often resuming their traditional polytheistic practices. This was not merely a matter of religious dissent; it was a full-scale political revolt challenging the very authority of the nascent Caliphate. Some tribes leveraged the opportunity to reassert their pre-Islamic dominance, while others were motivated by purely opportunistic reasons, seeking to capitalise on the power vacuum created by Muhammad(PBUH)'s death. The potential collapse of the Caliphate into a fractured collection of warring tribes posed a direct threat to the very survival of the burgeoning Islamic state.

Abu Bakr(RA)'s response was swift and decisive. He faced immense pressure to act decisively; inaction could embolden further defections and swiftly destabilise the fragile unity forged during the Prophet's lifetime. He refused to view the revolts as merely religious deviations but as a direct challenge to the political authority of the nascent Caliphate. His decision to use military force to quell the rebellions was not taken lightly. It marked a significant departure from the Prophet's primarily peaceful approach to spreading Islam, a strategic shift necessitated by the gravity of the situation. He understood that the survival of the nascent Islamic state depended on successfully suppressing these rebellions.

The military campaign was complex, demanding strategic acumen and logistical prowess. The Caliphate's resources were limited; the army was small, its manpower drawn from the recently unified tribes. The leadership faced challenges in equipment and logistics. The vastness of the Arabian Peninsula, with its challenging terrain and dispersed rebel groups, posed significant logistical hurdles. The campaign's success hinged upon effective communication, swift mobilisation, and astute military strategies. Moreover, the Caliphate had to address the potential for internal dissent and maintain the morale of its soldiers, who were fighting on diverse fronts against a formidable and decentralised enemy.

One of Abu Bakr(RA)'s most crucial decisions was the appointment of Khalid ibn al-Walid as army commander. Khalid, a seasoned and highly successful military strategist, recently converted to Islam. Though initially met with some resistance due to his past opposition to the Prophet, his appointment proved pivotal. Khalid's military genius and swift, decisive victories were instrumental in suppressing the rebellions. His understanding of desert warfare and ability to swiftly adapt his strategies were invaluable assets in the face of challenging terrain and dispersed enemy forces. His leadership instilled confidence and decisiveness among the Caliphate's troops, a much-needed factor considering their small size compared to the rebellion.

The Ridda Wars witnessed several key battles that shaped the course of the conflict. The battle of Yamama, for example, was particularly significant. The rebels in this region, led by the powerful Musaylima, presented a formidable challenge. Musaylima, known for his considerable military capabilities, challenged the Caliphate's authority on both religious and political grounds. He claimed prophethood, presenting a direct ideological threat to the burgeoning Islamic state. The battle was long and hard-fought, but ultimately resulted in a decisive Caliphate victory, primarily attributed to Khalid ibn al-Walid's tactical brilliance. This victory was a crucial turning point in the Ridda Wars, solidifying the Caliphate's control over a significant portion of the Arabian Peninsula.

The battles were not fought solely on the military front. Abu Bakr(RA) also employed sophisticated political maneuvering to weaken the rebels. He skillfully exploited existing tribal rivalries, forging alliances with certain groups against others, thereby minimising opposition to his forces. He offered amnesty to many tribes who surrendered peacefully, absorbing them back into the fold of the Caliphate. This strategic approach, alongside the military victories, helped to reduce the overall extent of the rebellions. The combination of military prowess and political acumen, demonstrated by Abu Bakr(RA) and Khalid ibn al-Walid, proved decisive in ensuring the survival of the Caliphate and shaping its future trajectory.

The Ridda Wars lasted approximately two years, during which the Caliphate's forces successfully suppressed most major rebellions. However, it's crucial to note that these wars were not entirely uniform; the uprisings and subsequent battles differed in scale and significance. While some were large-scale conflicts, others involved smaller-scale engagements. The challenges faced by the Caliphate's forces were multifold; they ranged from logistical difficulties and the vastness of the terrain to the necessity of handling diverse tribal allegiances and maintaining troop morale.

The consequences of the Ridda Wars were profound and far-reaching. The successful suppression of the rebellions effectively unified Arabia under the banner of the nascent Caliphate. It established the authority of the Caliphate not just through force of arms but also through political acumen and skilful negotiation. This unification, achieved after a tumultuous period of uncertainty, laid the foundation for the subsequent rapid expansion of the Islamic empire. The successful consolidation of power during these wars was instrumental in shaping the political landscape of the early Islamic world, allowing the Caliphate to move from a precarious position to one of considerable strength.

Furthermore, the wars significantly contributed to the standardisation and codification of Islamic practices. The diverse interpretations of Islam that surfaced during the rebellions and the need to unify the newly conquered territories led to a more systematic approach to religious law and practice. The standardisation of the Quran, undertaken under Abu Bakr(RA)'s leadership and continued by his successors, was directly linked to these events. Collecting and collating revelations from disparate sources, driven by the need for consistency and unity, cemented Islamic faith across the region. The political upheaval, therefore, contributed significantly to the theological and religious developments in the burgeoning Islamic world. The wars, hence, were not only a military conflict but a crucial moment in shaping the religious, political and social identity of the emerging Islamic world.

The Ridda Wars were a critical period in early Islamic history. The successful outcome, primarily attributed to the leadership of Abu Bakr(RA) and the military brilliance of Khalid ibn al-Walid, solidified the authority of the Caliphate and shaped the course of the nascent Islamic empire. The military victories and political shrewdness employed during these conflicts were not merely strategic maneuvers but crucial actions that determined the fate of the fledgling Muslim community. Despite the significant challenges posed by the sheer scale of the rebellions, the ability to unify diverse groups ultimately paved the way for the Islamic Golden Age, demonstrating the power of effective governance and decisive action in the face of adversity. The wars serve as a crucial case study of early state formation and the critical role of effective leadership in consolidating power and forging a lasting political entity from a fragile and diverse base. The legacy of this vital period resonates through subsequent centuries of Islamic history, underscoring the importance of unifying force and effective leadership in consolidating an emerging empire.

Administrative and Legal Reforms under Abu Bakr(RA)

Having successfully navigated the turbulent waters of the Ridda Wars, Abu Bakr(RA) faced the equally daunting task of establishing a stable and efficient administrative structure for the nascent Caliphate. The fragmented Arabian Peninsula, recently unified through military force, now required a robust system of governance to prevent a relapse into the chaos of pre-Islamic tribalism. This necessitated far-reaching administrative and legal reforms, which, though undertaken during a period of ongoing conflict, laid the foundation for the future growth and stability of the Islamic state.

One of the most significant challenges was the establishment of a standardised system of taxation. Before establishing the Caliphate, the Arabian Peninsula lacked a unified tax system. Each tribe operated autonomously, with its own resource allocation and revenue collection methods. This disparate system proved inadequate for the newly formed state, which required a reliable source of revenue to fund its growing military and administrative apparatus. Abu Bakr(RA), recognising this critical need, introduced a system of taxation based on the principles of Islamic jurisprudence. While precise details of the implementation vary in historical accounts, the core principles involved levying taxes on agricultural produce (Zakat), livestock, and other forms of wealth. This was not simply a matter of financial expediency; it was a critical step in consolidating the political authority of the Caliphate, asserting its control over economic resources across the previously independent tribes. Establishing a central treasury, managed by appointed officials, ensured the equitable distribution of these resources and facilitated the financing of essential government activities. This centralised fiscal system was crucial in supporting the ongoing military campaigns and administrative developments. Furthermore, it established a common purpose, linking various tribes through their shared contribution to the collective good. It established a fundamental principle of governance in the newly established state, a principle which would form a cornerstone for future fiscal policy.

Equally crucial was the reorganisation of the Caliphate's military. Though effective, the forces used to suppress the Ridda Wars were largely ad hoc. Abu Bakr(RA) understood that a standing army was essential for maintaining order and protecting the nascent state's borders. He established a more permanent, professionally organised military, drawing on the lessons learned during the recent conflicts. This involved recruiting and training soldiers and standardising military equipment, logistics, and command structure. The Caliphate's previous reliance on disparate tribal militias was replaced by a more centralised and disciplined fighting force, ensuring greater cohesion and effectiveness in future operations. The creation of this professional army was a cornerstone of Abu Bakr(RA)'s consolidation of power and expansionist ambitions. The professionalisation of the army wasn't just a military endeavour; it was a vital political step, reinforcing the Caliphate's authority and reducing reliance on potentially unreliable tribal loyalties. The creation of a centralised military was instrumental in the future expansion of the Islamic empire.

Beyond military and financial reforms, Abu Bakr(RA) actively sought to implement a uniform legal system. While Islamic law was not yet fully codified during his reign, he played a crucial role in establishing its fundamental principles as the basis for governance. Implementing Sharia, the Islamic law, was not a swift process but an evolutionary one built upon existing tribal customs and practices while introducing core elements of Islamic jurisprudence. This process involved consultation with leading scholars and jurists of the time, reflecting Abu Bakr(RA)'s emphasis on consensus-based decision-making. The implementation of Islamic law represented a significant departure from the pre-Islamic legal landscape of Arabia, consolidating the moral and legal frameworks of the Caliphate. This shift was crucial in strengthening the Caliphate's legitimacy and ensuring uniformity of governance across the diverse population it now governed. While the complete codification of Sharia would occur later, the groundwork laid by Abu Bakr(RA) significantly influenced the development of Islamic jurisprudence.

A critical aspect of Abu Bakr(RA)'s governance was his reliance on a council of advisors. He did not rule autocratically but engaged in extensive consultations with respected companions of the Prophet Muhammad(PBUH), relying on their knowledge and experience to guide his decisions. This consultative approach ensured broader acceptance of his policies and helped mitigate the potential for dissent within the community. This practice reflected the early Caliphate's commitment to inclusive governance, which contrasted sharply with later, more centralised forms of rule within the Islamic world. The key advisors' expertise covered a wide range of areas, including military strategy, legal matters, and financial administration, ensuring a diverse and informed perspective on critical matters of state.

Though sometimes fragmented, historical accounts offer glimpses into the practical implementation of Abu Bakr(RA)'s reforms. Primary sources, including the writings of early Islamic historians, reveal examples of the establishment of tax districts, the recruitment and training of soldiers, and the application of Islamic law in resolving disputes. While the exact methods and details may remain debated, it is clear that Abu Bakr(RA)'s reign was marked by significant administrative and legal innovation. These developments laid a crucial foundation for the future expansion and consolidation of the Caliphate, providing the organisational and legal framework for a rapidly expanding empire.

Abu Bakr(RA)'s administrative and legal reforms were not merely technical adjustments but fundamental steps in consolidating the political and social structure of the newly established Caliphate. They transcended the immediate challenges of post-prophetic leadership, shaping the long-term trajectory of the Islamic state. His approach, characterised by a blend of decisive action and careful consultation, created a robust system of governance that served as a blueprint for future Islamic empires. His reforms, though limited by the constraints of the era, laid the foundation for the remarkable growth and sophistication of governance and administration within the Islamic world. His legacy extends far beyond his short reign, demonstrating the lasting impact of thoughtful governance during the formative years of the early Islamic Caliphate. His emphasis on a centralised fiscal system, a professional army, and the framework for implementing Islamic law were all cornerstones of his legacy, profoundly influencing the development of the Islamic state and its enduring impact on the broader world. His legacy is a testament to the effectiveness of a blend of decisive leadership and inclusive governance. The principles he established during this critical juncture would shape the course of the Rashidun Caliphate and the broader development of Islamic governance for centuries to come. The groundwork laid during this period laid the foundation for the expansion and prosperity that characterised subsequent eras of Islamic history.

Economic Policies and Expansion Under Abu Bakr(RA)

The consolidation of power under Abu Bakr(RA) was inextricably linked to his economic policies and the early expansion of the Caliphate beyond the Arabian Peninsula. His reign witnessed the first significant military campaigns beyond the immediate confines of Arabia. These campaigns expanded the nascent Islamic state's territorial reach and fundamentally altered its economic landscape and administrative structure. The success of these initial conquests was not solely attributable to military prowess, but also to a shrewd understanding of financial management and the strategic integration of newly acquired territories.

One of the key elements of Abu Bakr(RA)'s economic strategy was the efficient management of the Zakat, the obligatory charitable levy prescribed in Islamic law. While Zakat existed in pre-Islamic Arabia in various forms, Abu Bakr(RA)'s administration standardised its collection and distribution, transforming it into a crucial instrument of religious observance and state finance. The Zakat, levied on agricultural produce, livestock, and other forms of wealth, provided a regular stream of revenue that significantly augmented the resources available to the Caliphate. This revenue was not simply hoarded but strategically deployed to fund the burgeoning military, support administrative functions, and provide essential welfare services within the expanding empire. Zakat's systematic collection and fair distribution were vital in fostering loyalty among the diverse populations under the Caliphate's rule. It was a powerful demonstration of the Islamic state's religious and practical benefits. Furthermore, the efficient management of Zakat contributed to economic stability and helped to alleviate potential grievances that could have led to social unrest.

The initial military campaigns under Abu Bakr(RA), primarily focused on consolidating the Arabian Peninsula and countering the threats posed by the Ridda (apostasy) movements, quickly transitioned into territorial expansion. These campaigns were undertaken not only for military and political reasons, but also to secure vital trade routes and access to resources. The conquest of Syria, in particular, was a watershed moment. Syria, at the time a critical part of the Byzantine Empire, possessed rich agricultural lands, flourishing trade networks, and strategically important cities. Its conquest drastically increased the Caliphate's economic potential. The acquisition of fertile farmland brought significant increases in food production, easing potential pressures caused by population growth within the expanding state. This newfound agricultural wealth provided a robust foundation for the Caliphate's expanding economy. The control of trade routes, particularly those leading to the Levant and beyond, also generated significant revenue through taxes and tolls, enriching the Caliphate's coffers.

Integrating newly conquered territories presented Abu Bakr(RA) and his successors with significant administrative challenges. Though largely dismantled, the existing Byzantine administrative apparatus provided a framework that could be adapted and integrated into the nascent Islamic state's system. The Caliphate's administration did not immediately impose a new system; instead, it adapted pre-existing structures and processes wherever possible, minimising disruption and fostering a smoother transition for the conquered populations. This pragmatic approach helped avoid widespread resistance and fostered a degree of cooperation that accelerated the integration process. However, the practicalities of governing such diverse populations required a sophisticated and responsive administrative structure. The early Caliphate grappled with questions of taxation, land ownership, and the legal rights of conquered peoples. Establishing a centralised financial system was critical to managing the influx of revenue from newly acquired territories. This involved developing sophisticated record-keeping, accounting, and tax collection methods, demanding a growing administrative bureaucracy.

The initial expansion under Abu Bakr(RA) also had profound implications for the lives of the conquered populations. While the early Caliphate was noted for its relatively tolerant policies towards non-Muslims, particularly those who paid the jizya (a poll tax), the conquered peoples nonetheless found themselves under a new political and economic order. While the specifics varied according to the context of each conquered region, the general aim was the incorporation of conquered territories into the Caliphate's financial and administrative structure. This meant existing tax systems were often adapted or replaced by those aligned with Islamic law principles. Land ownership, a highly complex issue in many conquered regions, was also subject to review and re-allocation. While some communities benefited from increased economic stability and opportunities, others faced adjustments to their traditional ways of life. While sometimes fraught with tensions, these changes ultimately contributed to the Caliphate's capacity for sustaining long-term economic growth.

The economic consequences of expansion were multi-faceted. The increase in available resources fueled the growth of the Caliphate's military and administrative apparatus. The influx of wealth from conquered territories provided funds for public works projects, the construction of infrastructure, and the support of religious and educational institutions. Establishing new trade routes and access to markets beyond the Arabian Peninsula spurred economic activity and fostered the development of trade networks that linked distant regions. The influx of goods and services from conquered areas significantly diversified the Caliphate's economy. However, this period also witnessed the emergence of new economic challenges. The administration needed to manage the complexities of a vast and diverse economy, dealing with differing economic systems, taxation methods, and currency exchanges. The administration had to find ways to ensure that the revenues generated by the expansion could be channelled effectively to fund the expanding bureaucracy and military, while preventing corruption and inequitable distribution of wealth.

The early expansion under Abu Bakr(RA) laid the foundations for the later, more extensive conquests under Umar(RA) ibn al-Khattab. The administrative and economic systems established during Abu Bakr(RA)'s reign provided a framework for the subsequent management of an empire that stretched across vast swathes of the Middle East and beyond. The initial successes in consolidating power within Arabia and securing initial expansion provided a springboard for the early Islamic Caliphate's further territorial growth and economic prosperity. The efficient management of resources, the strategic integration of conquered territories, and the development of a competent administrative structure were all essential aspects of Abu Bakr(RA)'s contribution. His economic policies and approach to incorporating newly acquired territories were critical components in ensuring the long-term success of the Rashidun Caliphate. The integration of conquered regions was a military accomplishment and a crucial economic and political engineering feat that shaped early

Islamic history. The economic and administrative structures implemented during this period shaped the development of the Islamic world for centuries to come. The legacy of Abu Bakr(RA)'s economic policies and the early expansion of the Caliphate continue to be a subject of significant scholarly interest, highlighting the enduring importance of understanding the foundations of the early Islamic state.

Legacy of Abu Bakr(RA) and the Transition to Umar(RA)

Abu Bakr(RA)'s death in 634 CE marked a pivotal moment in the history of the nascent Islamic Caliphate. His eleven-month reign, though brief, left an indelible mark, laying the groundwork for the subsequent expansion and consolidation of the newly established state. His legacy extended beyond the immediate military successes in quelling the Ridda wars and initiating the conquests of Syria and Iraq. He established crucial administrative and legal precedents, shaping the Rashidun Caliphate's fundamental institutions. His success lay not only in his military acumen but also in his ability to build consensus, manage diverse populations, and create a system of governance that could adapt to the challenges of rapid expansion.

Abu Bakr(RA)'s most significant achievement was the standardisation of the Quran. Before his Caliphate, the revelations of the Prophet Muhammad(PBUH) existed in scattered fragments, compiled by individual scribes and memorised by various companions. Recognising the potential for discord and misinterpretations, Abu Bakr(RA) initiated a project to collect and compile these scattered verses into a single, unified text. This task fell to Zayd ibn Thabit, a renowned scribe and companion of the Prophet, who meticulously gathered and collated the verses, ensuring the textual integrity of the holy scripture. This monumental undertaking, completed during Abu Bakr(RA)'s reign, established a definitive version of the Quran, a cornerstone of Islamic faith and identity. The compilation not only resolved potential disputes over the content of the Quran but also provided a unifying force for the diverse community of Muslims, solidifying the religious foundation of the Caliphate. This crucial step in solidifying the religious identity of the newly formed Caliphate laid the groundwork for its social and political unity. Therefore, the standardisation of the Quran went beyond a mere textual exercise; it constituted a profound act of political and religious consolidation.

Beyond the religious sphere, Abu Bakr(RA)'s legacy also manifested in his administrative reforms. While the existing tribal structures of Arabia provided a starting point for governance, Abu Bakr(RA)'s administration recognised the need for a more centralised and efficient system to manage the expanding empire. He established a centralised system of tax collection, mainly based on the pre-existing Zakat system. Still, he adapted and expanded to meet the needs of a larger and more diverse population. While rooted in Islamic principles, this system was also practically oriented, ensuring a stable flow of revenue to support the burgeoning military and administrative apparatus. The efficient collection and distribution of Zakat funded the state. They fostered a sense of shared responsibility and collective identity among Muslims, contributing to the stability and cohesion of the early Caliphate. His attention to detail in economic management was instrumental in his success. He established a robust system of accounting and record-keeping, a vital tool for managing the state's financial resources and ensuring transparency and accountability.

The selection of Umar(RA) ibn al-Khattab as Abu Bakr(RA)'s successor was a significant event, illustrating the process of leadership transition in the early Islamic state. Unlike hereditary succession, common in many contemporary empires, the Rashidun Caliphate adhered to a more consultative approach. The process involved a Shura, a council of prominent companions of the Prophet, who deliberated and ultimately selected Umar(RA) through consensus-building and mutual agreement. The selection of Umar(RA), a renowned companion known for his piety, wisdom, and administrative capabilities, highlighted the importance of meritocracy and consensus in the early Islamic system of governance. Though not consistently smooth in later succession crises, this process established a crucial precedent for choosing leaders based on their qualities rather than their lineage.

Umar(RA)'s ascension to power marked a notable shift in leadership style compared to Abu Bakr(RA). While Abu Bakr(RA)'s approach was characterised by diplomacy, consensus-building and a focus on consolidating the existing infrastructure, Umar(RA) was known for his decisiveness, stringent administration, and focus on expansion. While both leaders shared a deep commitment to Islamic principles, their methods differed considerably. Umar(RA), often described as a strict and even austere ruler, implemented significant reforms in various aspects of governance, particularly in the administrative and military realms. His reign was defined by a relentless expansion of the Caliphate, extending its reach across vast swathes of the Middle East and beyond. His administrative prowess helped manage the challenges posed by this rapid growth, creating a more formalised administrative structure and codifying various aspects of Islamic law.

The comparison between Abu Bakr(RA) and Umar(RA) reveals contrasting yet complementary aspects of leadership in the early Caliphate. Abu Bakr(RA) focused on consolidating the foundations, laying the groundwork for a stable and unified state. He prioritised consensus-building and internal stability. On the other hand, Umar(RA) focused on expansion, building upon the foundations laid by his predecessor. He employed a more assertive and centralised form of governance. While Abu Bakr(RA)'s reign was marked by diplomacy and internal cohesion, Umar(RA)'s reign exemplified decisive action and territorial expansion. Both leaders, however, shared a common commitment to justice, religious piety, and the welfare of their subjects. Despite their different styles, the smooth transition from one to the other highlighted the institutional stability of the early Caliphate and the flexibility of its governance system.

The administrative changes under Umar(RA) were substantial. He further developed the centralised administrative system, creating more defined bureaucratic structures and standardising procedures. He established a postal service for communication throughout the empire, a critical innovation for coordinating administrative activities and maintaining effective control over distant provinces. Umar(RA)'s implementation of a standardised currency further enhanced the Caliphate's economic efficiency. This eased trade and financial transactions across the vast and diverse regions under Caliphate control. He also reformed the tax system, implementing stricter measures to ensure fair and equitable collection. His administrative reforms were instrumental in managing the complexities of governing a vast and expanding empire, providing stability and efficiency. His pragmatic approach and strong leadership enabled the Caliphate to manage growth challenges and consolidate its position as a significant regional power.

Umar(RA)'s military campaigns were perhaps the most visible aspect of his rule. His campaigns resulted in significant territorial gains, expanding the Caliphate's reach into Persia (Sasanian Empire), Egypt (Byzantine Empire), and other regions. These conquests were not simply acts of military aggression; they were also strategic moves aimed at securing vital trade routes and resources and consolidating the power of the Caliphate in the region. The successes of these campaigns, however, were not solely military. Umar(RA)'s effective administrative strategies were crucial in securing and integrating the newly conquered territories into the Caliphate. He dispatched governors to administer the conquered lands, ensuring the implementation of fair policies and a degree of local autonomy. His attention to the welfare of both Muslims and non-Muslims within the conquered territories helped maintain stability and integrate them into the broader political and economic system of the Caliphate. His pragmatic approach to governance, balancing the need for centralised control with respect for local customs, ensured the long-term sustainability of the empire.

The transition from Abu Bakr(RA) to Umar(RA) is crucial in early Islamic history. It marked not merely a change of leadership but also a shift in governance styles while maintaining a commitment to the fundamental principles of the early Caliphate. Abu Bakr(RA)'s focus on consolidation and consensus provided a stable foundation upon which Umar(RA) built his ambitious expansion and administrative reform program. Although distinct, the combination of their leadership styles proved remarkably effective in establishing a powerful and enduring empire. The legacy of both leaders shaped the trajectory of the Rashidun Caliphate and continues to inform discussions about leadership, governance, and religious authority in the Islamic world. Their actions and policies provided a model for subsequent Islamic rulers, illustrating the complexities and challenges of building and maintaining a large and diverse empire based on principles of faith and justice. Studying their reigns offers invaluable insights into the dynamics of early Islamic governance, religious development, and the political and economic transformations that shaped the early Muslim world.

Chapter 2
Umar(RA) ibn al-Khattab: Consolidation and Expansion of the Caliphate

Umar's(RA)'s Administrative Reforms and Centralized Governance

Umar(RA) ibn al-Khattab's ascension to the caliphate in 634 CE marked a significant turning point in the history of the early Islamic state. While Abu Bakr(RA) had laid the foundations for a centralised administration, Umar(RA) undertook a comprehensive restructuring, transforming the nascent Caliphate into a highly organised and efficient governing entity capable of managing its rapidly expanding territories. His reforms were far-reaching, encompassing military organisation, financial administration, legal frameworks, and the establishment of a sophisticated bureaucratic apparatus. These changes were crucial in consolidating the Caliphate's power and ensuring long-term stability.

One of Umar(RA)'s most significant contributions was the creation of a robust centralised bureaucracy. Unlike Abu Bakr(RA)'s era's relatively informal administrative structures, Umar(RA) established a system of clearly defined offices and responsibilities. He appointed highly skilled and trusted individuals to key positions, often selecting individuals based on their merit and piety rather than their tribal affiliations. This meritocratic approach helped to mitigate the potential for tribal conflicts and ensured that competent individuals staffed the administration. Establishing a formalised bureaucracy was not simply a matter of administrative efficiency; it represented a profound shift in governance within the Caliphate, moving away from a more loosely structured tribal system towards a more centralised and formalised state structure.

Establishing provinces, known as *wilayat*, was a cornerstone of Umar(RA)'s administrative reforms. As the Caliphate expanded rapidly through military conquests, the need for efficient governance in conquered territories became paramount. Umar(RA) divided the empire into strategically organised provinces, each placed under the authority of a governor (*wali*). These governors were not merely military commanders; they were responsible for the overall administration of their respective provinces, overseeing tax collection, justice, and the maintenance of order. The selection of *wali*s was a matter of great care; Umar(RA) often personally interviewed candidates, assessing their character, competence, and commitment to justice. He emphasised the importance of piety and fairness in their governance, instructing them to treat Muslims and non-Muslims justly and equitably.

The effectiveness of the *wilayat* system depended heavily on efficient communication and information flow. Recognising this, Umar(RA) established a sophisticated postal system, connecting the various provinces to the capital in Medina. This system, a remarkable innovation for its time, facilitated rapid communication between the central government and the provincial administrations. Couriers, traversing vast distances on camelback, relayed messages, reports, and official decrees, ensuring that the central government maintained effective control over its vast territories. This system was not merely a logistical achievement; it was fundamental to the political stability and cohesion of the expanding empire. Without it, maintaining effective control over the outlying regions would have been nearly impossible.

Umar(RA)'s administrative reforms also encompassed the financial management of the Caliphate. He developed a more formalised taxation system, streamlining the collection and distribution of revenues. Building upon the Zakat system, he implemented a more comprehensive system, encompassing taxes levied on conquered territories. This system was designed to be efficient and equitable, ensuring that revenues were collected fairly and used effectively to fund the state's activities. The revenue generated was vital for maintaining the military and financing public works projects, supporting the poor and needy, and ensuring the overall welfare of the population. Umar(RA)'s meticulous attention to financial matters ensured the economic stability and prosperity of the Caliphate. He introduced a strict accounting and record-keeping system, ensuring transparency and accountability in the management of public funds. This contributed significantly to the avoidance of corruption and the efficient allocation of resources.

Implementing a standardised currency was another significant achievement of Umar(RA)'s administrative reforms. Before his reign, the Caliphate used various currencies, creating trade and financial transaction complexities. Umar(RA) introduced a unified currency, facilitating trade and economic activity across the expanding empire. This standardisation simplified economic transactions, reduced costs associated with currency exchange, and enhanced the overall economic efficiency of the Caliphate. Introducing a unified currency eased economic transactions and symbolised the Caliphate's centralised authority and ability to integrate disparate regions under a unified financial system.

Beyond financial management, Umar(RA)'s reforms extended to the judicial system. He emphasised the importance of justice and fairness in his administration, instructing governors and judges to adhere strictly to Islamic law. He established a more formalised system of courts, ensuring that disputes were resolved efficiently and equitably. His focus on justice and the rule of law was crucial in maintaining order and stability within the expanding empire, helping to build trust and confidence among the diverse populations under Caliphate rule. He also established a system for handling complaints and grievances from the population, ensuring that the concerns of ordinary citizens received attention and redress. This system helped to limit the potential for social unrest and strengthened the legitimacy of the Caliphate's authority.

The appointment of judges and other officials was done with a great deal of care and attention to detail. Umar(RA) personally vetted many candidates, ensuring they possessed the requisite piety, knowledge of Islamic law, and impartiality. He also provided clear guidelines for the conduct of officials, instructing them to uphold justice and fairness in all their dealings. He emphasised the importance of integrity and accountability, ensuring that wrongdoing would be met with swift and decisive punishment. This strict approach helped to minimise corruption and maintain a high standard of ethical conduct within the administration. This emphasis on competency and moral character was instrumental in building a strong and effective bureaucracy.

The administrative structure under Umar(RA) was remarkably efficient considering the vastness of the Caliphate. The combination of centralised authority, a sophisticated communication network, a standardised currency, a well-defined judicial system, and a meritocratic selection process created a governing system capable of managing the enormous complexities of an expanding empire. However, it's crucial to acknowledge that this system was not without its challenges despite its effectiveness. The sheer scale of the empire and the vast distances involved posed logistical difficulties. Furthermore, integrating diverse populations with different legal and cultural traditions presented significant hurdles.

Nevertheless, Umar(RA)'s administrative reforms were a landmark achievement in early Islamic history, laying the groundwork for the later development of Islamic governance. His focus on centralisation, efficiency, and justice created a state apparatus capable of handling the complexities of a vast and diverse empire. While his reign was marked by military expansion, it was equally shaped by his profound and lasting contributions to developing a sophisticated and efficient administrative system. His legacy as a strong and just ruler, known for his piety and dedication to the welfare of his subjects, cemented his place as one of the most significant figures in the history of the Rashidun Caliphate. His reforms established a model of centralised governance that influenced subsequent Islamic empires and continues to be studied and analysed by historians and political scientists today. His innovations in administration were instrumental in establishing the long-term stability and success of the early Islamic state. The systems he put in place—from the postal service to the standardised currency and formalised judiciary—represent significant milestones in developing effective governance in a complex and rapidly expanding empire. His enduring legacy lies in his ability to create a system that managed territorial expansion and internal cohesion, a crucial aspect of early Islamic history.

Military Conquests During Umar(RA)'s Reign

Umar(RA)'s reign witnessed a dramatic expansion of the nascent Islamic Caliphate, fueled by a series of brilliant military campaigns. Building upon the foundations laid by Abu Bakr(RA) during the Ridda Wars, Umar(RA)'s caliphate saw the systematic conquest of the vast Sasanian Persian Empire and further advances in the Byzantine Levant. These conquests were not merely opportunistic raids but the result of meticulously planned and executed military strategies, reflecting a sophisticated understanding of logistics, strategy, and the effective utilisation of existing military expertise.

Central to Umar(RA)'s military successes was the continuation and refinement of the effective army organisation inherited from his predecessor. While Abu Bakr(RA) had successfully united the various Arab tribes under a single banner, Umar(RA) further consolidated this unity by creating a more formalised and hierarchical military structure. This structure moved beyond the reliance on tribal allegiances, fostering a more cohesive and professional fighting force. The selection of commanders was based on merit, demonstrating a shrewd recognition that military prowess, strategic acumen, and loyalty to the Caliphate were far more critical than tribal affiliations.

Khalid ibn al-Walid's role in these conquests was pivotal. His tactical brilliance and strategic foresight had already been instrumental during the Ridda Wars, and Umar(RA) wisely retained him as one of his principal commanders. Khalid's leadership, marked by his tactical flexibility, rapid decision-making, and ability to inspire his troops, proved invaluable during the campaigns in Persia and Syria. His innovative battlefield tactics, particularly his mastery of swift maneuvers and flanking movements, often resulted in decisive victories against numerically superior forces. His reputation as a peerless military leader instilled confidence in his soldiers, fostering a fighting spirit crucial to succeeding in the face of formidable opposition. However, even Khalid's successes were not solely a matter of individual brilliance but depended on the broader support of Umar(RA)'s centralised and efficient administrative system.

The conquest of Persia, a vast and powerful empire, presented a significant military challenge. Although weakened by internal strife and prior conflicts, the Sasanian army remained formidable. Umar(RA)'s strategy involved a combination of carefully planned offensives, taking advantage of the Sasanians' weakened state and internal divisions, and a gradual but relentless advance. The battles of al-Qādisiyyah (636 CE) and Nahavand (642 CE) proved crucial turning points. At al-Qādisiyyah, the Muslim forces, under the leadership of Saad ibn Abi Waqqas, after some initial setbacks, achieved a decisive victory against the Sasanian army, shattering the backbone of their military power. The battle demonstrated the effectiveness of the Islamic armies' combined arms tactics, integrating cavalry and infantry effectively. Using catapults and siege warfare in various campaigns further showed the army's adaptability. The subsequent victory at Nahavand effectively dismantled the remaining Sasanian resistance, paving the way for the conquest of the entire Persian Empire.

The conquests were not without significant challenges. The Sasanian Empire possessed a vast and complex administrative system, a highly trained army, and a deeply entrenched culture. The initial resistance was often fierce, and the Islamic armies faced strong opposition from highly disciplined and well-equipped Sasanian troops. The terrain varied significantly across the conquered territories, posing logistical difficulties for the supply lines. Maintaining communication and coordination across this expansive battlefield was crucial and, although successful, presented significant challenges. But the Muslim armies' capacity to adapt and learn from experience, impressive fighting skills, and strong morale allowed them to overcome these obstacles.

The conquest of Persia was not only a military achievement but also a significant geopolitical event. It marked the end of the long-standing Sasanian Empire, a major player on the world stage for centuries. The acquisition of such a vast and wealthy territory dramatically increased the resources available to the Caliphate, enriching its treasury and expanding its influence. The immense wealth and resources poured into the coffers of the Caliphate fueled further expansion, strengthening the military apparatus and developing infrastructure and administration within the newly conquered territories.

Concurrently with the conquests in Persia, the Muslim armies continued their advance in the Levant, taking advantage of the internal weaknesses within the Byzantine Empire. Under the leadership of generals such as Abu Ubaidah ibn al-Jarrah and Amr ibn al-As, the Muslim armies achieved a string of victories, culminating in the capture of Damascus (634/5 CE) and Jerusalem (637 CE). The campaigns in the Levant also benefited from excellent battlefield strategy, demonstrating the Muslim armies' ability to adapt to different terrains and enemy tactics. The battles against the Byzantines involved numerous sieges and complex maneuvers, highlighting the military's sophisticated understanding of siege warfare and tactics.

The capture of Jerusalem holds particular significance. The city was a major religious centre, and its capture marked a turning point in the relationship between the newly emerging Caliphate and the Christian population under its expanding sway. Umar(RA)'s visit to the city and his treatment of the Christian inhabitants established a precedent for the Caliphate's relatively tolerant administration of conquered territories with significant non-Muslim populations.

The integration of the conquered territories into the Caliphate was a complex process. Umar(RA)'s administrative reforms were crucial in governing these newly acquired regions. He established a system of provinces, appointing governors responsible for maintaining order, collecting taxes, and ensuring the smooth functioning of the administration. He adopted a pragmatic approach towards the non-Muslim populations, essentially maintaining existing administrative structures and systems where appropriate, while gradually incorporating the conquered territories into the broader administrative apparatus of the Caliphate.

The challenges of integrating these diverse populations were considerable. Differences in language, culture, religion, and legal systems required a delicate balance of policies, avoiding any action that could provoke widespread unrest. While establishing a unified currency, as previously noted, had immense economic implications, standardising legal systems, religious practices, and administrative structures across such a vast and diverse expanse was a gradual process that spanned beyond Umar(RA)'s reign. The treatment of non-Muslim populations, however, remained a notable aspect of the Caliphate's early policy, often involving a form of religious tolerance and granting certain rights, although the specifics varied over time and place.

In conclusion, the military conquests during Umar(RA)'s reign were pivotal in developing the early Islamic Caliphate. The success of these campaigns, underpinned by sound military strategy, astute leadership, and

Umar(RA)'s effective administrative reforms, laid the foundation for the further expansion and consolidation of Islamic rule across vast territories in the Middle East. The efficient organisation of the army and administration ensured the newly acquired territories were successfully integrated into the Caliphate. However, the complexities of this integration would continue to be addressed by subsequent rulers. The victories and the ensuing consolidation of power significantly shaped the region's political, social, and economic landscape, creating an environment that would influence the course of history for centuries to come. Therefore, the military triumphs of this era cannot be separated from the concurrent administrative and political innovations that ensured the stability and longevity of the Caliphate's expansion.

Economic Policies and Infrastructure Development Under Umar(RA)

Umar(RA) ibn al-Khattab's reign, while marked by dramatic military expansion, was equally characterised by a shrewd and pragmatic approach to economic management. Unlike many conquering empires prioritising the immediate extraction of wealth from conquered territories, Umar(RA)'s policies emphasised fiscal responsibility, equitable distribution of resources, and long-term economic stability. This approach proved crucial in consolidating the newly acquired territories and fostering a sense of security and prosperity among the diverse populations under the Caliphate's rule. His economic vision extended beyond mere revenue generation; it encompassed the development of infrastructure that would support sustained economic growth and enhance the overall well-being of his subjects.

A cornerstone of Umar(RA)'s economic strategy was his unwavering commitment to fiscal prudence and transparency. He inherited a treasury enriched by the spoils of war, but he resisted the temptation to squander this newfound wealth on lavish projects or personal enrichment. Instead, he established a rigorous accounting system and meticulous record-keeping, ensuring that all revenues were accounted for and disbursed according to established principles. This commitment to transparency fostered public trust and confidence in the Caliphate's financial administration. Umar(RA)'s frugality further reinforced this message, setting an example for his officials and demonstrating his dedication to serving the public interest. His simple lifestyle contrasted sharply with the opulent displays of wealth often associated with rulers, solidifying his image as a just and equitable leader.

The equitable distribution of resources was another defining feature of Umar(RA)'s economic policies. He established a taxation system designed to be fair and proportionate, considering the capacity of different individuals and communities to contribute. The taxation system, while drawing upon existing Sasanian and Byzantine models, was adapted to the specific circumstances of the Islamic Caliphate, emphasising the principles of justice and equity. The zakat, a mandatory form of charity in Islam, was significant in redistributing wealth, supporting the poor and needy, and fostering social cohesion. Umar(RA) ensured the consistent and impartial implementation of zakat, ensuring its effective use in alleviating poverty and supporting vulnerable segments of society. This systematic approach to wealth redistribution not only addressed social inequalities but also contributed to the overall stability of the Caliphate by reducing social unrest and enhancing social harmony.

Furthermore, Umar(RA) implemented policies designed to stimulate economic activity and promote trade. He recognised the vital role of commerce in fostering prosperity and ensuring the financial well-being of his subjects. He standardised weights and measures across the vast territories under his rule, eliminating inconsistencies that hampered trade and discouraged fair commercial practices. This standardisation promoted transparency and facilitated transactions, fostering a more robust and efficient marketplace. The development of a unified currency also played a crucial role in streamlining trade and facilitating economic interactions across the diverse regions of the Caliphate. This facilitated internal trade and eased economic interactions within the expanding territories. This unified economic framework further solidified the integration of the newly conquered territories into the Caliphate.

Recognising the importance of infrastructure in supporting economic growth, Umar(RA) initiated ambitious public works projects that transformed the landscape of the Caliphate. He oversaw the construction of a vast network of roads, facilitating trade, communication, and the movement of troops. These roads were not mere pathways but strategically planned routes designed to connect key economic centres, ensuring efficient movement of goods and people across the expanded empire. These infrastructure developments served financial and military purposes, strengthening the Caliphate's capacity for trade, military movements, and administration.

Beyond roads, Umar(RA) invested heavily in the development of irrigation systems. The expansion of agriculture was vital for the economic self-sufficiency of the Caliphate. His focus on improving irrigation enhanced agricultural productivity, resulting in increased food production, surplus for trade, and food security. By systematically improving existing irrigation systems and building new ones, he expanded the cultivable land and increased crop yields. This strategic investment in irrigation not only contributed to the economic prosperity of the Caliphate but also enhanced its stability by ensuring a consistent food supply. The increased agricultural productivity also had significant socio-economic implications, reducing reliance on imported food, stimulating regional economies, and fostering greater self-sufficiency across the Caliphate.

The construction of public buildings, such as mosques, hospitals, and other public facilities, further underscored Umar(RA)'s commitment to infrastructure development. These projects generated employment opportunities, stimulated local economies, and improved the quality of life for the citizenry. Mosques, in particular, served as places of worship and community centres, fostering social cohesion and providing a sense of shared identity across diverse communities. The strategic placement of these buildings further underlined the Caliphate's attempt at integrating the diverse populations and fostering a collective identity.

Umar(RA)'s economic policies were not solely focused on large-scale projects. He also implemented policies aimed at improving the lives of ordinary citizens. He implemented measures to alleviate poverty and improve access to essential resources, addressing social justice and economic equity issues. This approach reduced the likelihood of social unrest and enhanced social cohesion, providing a more stable foundation for his expansionist policies. By supporting the poor and promoting social justice, he ensured that the benefits of economic growth were not concentrated in the hands of a small elite but were more broadly distributed across society. This promoted a sense of shared prosperity and lessened the potential for social instability that could threaten the stability of the burgeoning Caliphate.

The success of Umar(RA)'s economic policies is evident in the unprecedented growth and prosperity that the Caliphate experienced during his reign. His emphasis on fiscal responsibility, equitable distribution of resources, and strategic infrastructure development created a robust and resilient economy that could sustain the ongoing military expansion and the integration of diverse conquered territories. The resulting economic stability laid the foundation for the Caliphate's continued growth and influence in the following decades. His policies, which blended pragmatism, foresight and an understanding of the socio-economic realities of his time, served as a model for subsequent rulers and left a lasting impact on the economic development of the early Islamic world.

Dr. Shaikh Mohammad Shahriyar Wahab

The legacy of Umar(RA)'s economic policies extended far beyond his lifetime. His emphasis on fiscal responsibility and transparent governance became a benchmark for future rulers, influencing the administrative practices of the Caliphate for generations to come. The infrastructure projects he initiated, particularly the road networks and irrigation systems, continued to benefit the region for centuries, shaping the economic and social landscapes of the conquered territories. His commitment to social justice and equitable distribution of resources left a lasting imprint on Islamic governance, reinforcing the ideal of a just and equitable society. His methods of balancing the needs of the state with the well-being of his subjects became a central theme in the discussion of just governance in the Islamic world.

In conclusion, Umar(RA) ibn al-Khattab's economic policies were integral to the success of his reign. His pragmatic and visionary approach to economic management, characterised by fiscal prudence, equitable distribution, and large-scale infrastructural development, fostered unprecedented economic growth and stability within the rapidly expanding Caliphate. His legacy is a testament to the significance of sound economic policies in shaping history, demonstrating how strategic economic planning can contribute to a burgeoning empire's long-term prosperity and stability. His reign is a significant case study in the intersection of political and economic strategies in early Islamic history, illustrating how effective economic governance can contribute to military success and lasting socio-economic progress. The lasting impact of Umar(RA)'s policies underscores the enduring relevance of his economic vision for understanding the complexities of early Islamic governance and its enduring legacy.

Legal and Judicial Systems under Umar(RA)

Umar(RA) ibn al-Khattab's reign witnessed not only significant military expansion but also a profound reorganisation and standardisation of the legal and judicial systems within the nascent Islamic Caliphate. Before his caliphate, the application of Islamic law, primarily based on the Quran and the Sunnah (prophetic traditions), was often inconsistent and varied regionally, reflecting the diverse legal customs and traditions inherited from the Byzantine and Sasanian empires. Umar(RA)'s pragmatic approach sought to unify and systematise this legal landscape, creating a more cohesive and equitable justice system across the expanding territories.

One of the key aspects of Umar(RA)'s legal reforms was the emphasis on codifying existing legal practices. While a complete codification of Islamic law would only occur later in Islamic history, Umar(RA) initiated several crucial steps towards this goal. He recognised the need to address the increasing complexity of legal issues arising from the rapid expansion of the Caliphate and the diverse population it now encompassed. This necessitated a more structured and systematic approach to legal matters than the earlier, more ad hoc methods. Before his time, the absence of a comprehensive written code meant that legal rulings often relied on scholarly interpretations of the Quran and Sunnah, leading to potential inconsistencies and disputes. Umar(RA) understood that a more standardised approach was necessary to maintain social order and ensure equitable justice.

The focus on codification under Umar(RA) did not involve a systematic writing of a complete legal code in the way that we understand legal codes today. Instead, it centred on documenting legal precedents and rulings, assembling collections of judicial decisions, and establishing clear guidelines for applying Islamic law in various contexts. This approach reflected the prevailing understanding of Islamic law as a dynamic and evolving system, drawing upon both revealed texts (Quran and Sunnah) and established scholarly interpretation. This method, however, allowed for a greater degree of consistency and predictability in applying law across the growing empire.

Central to Umar(RA)'s legal reforms was establishing a structured judicial system. While rudimentary forms of dispute resolution existed before his reign, Umar(RA) formalised the process by establishing courts (qada) and appointing judges (qadis). These courts were not simply places for resolving disputes but also crucial for implementing and interpreting the law. The selection of

Qadis was of considerable importance. Umar(RA) emphasised choosing individuals known for their piety, legal knowledge, and fairness. He established specific criteria for their appointment, striving to ensure that those entrusted with the administration of justice possessed the necessary qualities of integrity and competence. The aim was to create a system where justice would be served and perceived as impartially and fairly delivered. This ensured some level of standardised legal practices, though regional variation remained.

The process of dispute resolution under Umar(RA)'s system involved a structured approach. It started with attempts at conciliation and mediation, reflecting the Islamic emphasis on resolving disputes peacefully. If these efforts failed, the matter would proceed to court. The qadi would hear evidence from both sides, consider relevant Islamic legal principles, and render a judgment. Appeals were possible under certain circumstances, offering a mechanism for reviewing decisions. The system was not without imperfections, particularly given the geographical vastness of the Caliphate and the logistical challenges of maintaining communication and consistency across such a wide area. However, establishing clear procedures and guidelines contributed to more order and predictability in the judicial process.

To ensure the judicial system's integrity, Umar(RA) implemented measures to prevent corruption and ensure accountability. He emphasised transparency in judicial proceedings and held qadis accountable for their decisions. This included mechanisms for reviewing their performance and addressing complaints against them. Umar(RA)'s involvement in overseeing the judicial system reinforced its importance and his commitment to justice. His actions served as a model and underscored the central role of justice in the functioning of the Caliphate.

Historical sources offer glimpses into specific legal cases and judicial processes during Umar(RA)'s reign. While detailed records are scarce, these accounts reveal the practical application of Islamic law and the efforts to ensure fairness and equity. For instance, disputes over land ownership, inheritance issues, and commercial transactions were resolved through the judicial system. These cases often illustrate the principles of Islamic law, such as the importance of evidence, the role of witnesses, and the application of the equitable tenets in resolving disputes. Focusing on fairness and justice was paramount in Umar(RA)'s reign and shaped his judicial decisions.

Establishing a standardised system of weights and measures under Umar(RA) had significant legal ramifications. The inconsistencies in weights and measures across different regions have resulted in numerous disputes and fraud. By standardising weights and measures, Umar(RA) facilitated trade and helped resolve conflicts arising from discrepancies in commercial transactions. This created a more equitable economic environment and reduced litigation related to commercial disputes. The standardisation was critical in minimising fraud and enforcing fair trade practices, thereby strengthening the integrity of the legal and economic systems.

Umar(RA)'s reforms also extended to the realm of criminal justice. He ensured that punishments were applied fairly and consistently, according to Islamic law. While the Quran prescribed specific punishments for certain crimes, Umar(RA)'s policies aimed to provide these punishments, which were used judiciously and with consideration for the particular circumstances of each case. The focus on equitable application, even within the framework of prescribed punishments, underscored the commitment to justice. This did not imply an absence of harsh penalties, but rather an attempt to administer these within a framework of fairness and proportionality.

The expansion of the Caliphate posed significant challenges to the administration of justice. The diversity of populations within the conquered territories brought about different legal customs and traditions. Umar(RA)'s approach sought to balance the application of Islamic law with respect for existing customs and practices that did not contradict fundamental Islamic principles. This pragmatic approach aimed at avoiding unnecessary conflict while gradually integrating the conquered populations into the broader legal framework of the Caliphate. The gradual integration process reflected the realities of governing a diverse and geographically extensive empire.

Despite the efforts towards unification and standardisation, inconsistencies and regional variations remained in the application of Islamic law during Umar(RA)'s reign. The vastness of the Caliphate and the challenges of communication and administration across diverse regions made it difficult to ensure complete uniformity. However,

Umar(RA)'s initiatives represented a significant step toward creating a more structured and equitable justice system within the early Islamic state. His reforms laid the foundation for future developments in Islamic jurisprudence and the evolution of legal systems in the Muslim world. Though imperfect in their complete implementation, the efforts made in his reign mark a watershed moment in the early development of Islamic law and its institutionalisation within the growing Caliphate. The legacy of his judicial reforms continued to shape the legal and administrative structures of subsequent Islamic states, highlighting the enduring impact of his pragmatic yet visionary approach to establishing a just and equitable society. The focus on fairness, accountability and an apparent attempt at codifying and implementing legal structures continues to influence the legal systems in many regions today.

The Legacy of Umar(RA) and the Transition to Uthman(RA)

Umar(RA)'s death, by assassination in 644 CE, marked a profound turning point in the history of the early Caliphate. His assassination, a brutal act committed by a disgruntled Persian slave named Abu Lulu' al-Majusi, not only deprived the nascent Islamic state of its highly effective leader but also exposed underlying tensions and vulnerabilities within the burgeoning empire. Umar(RA)'s twelve-year reign had been defined by remarkable expansion, administrative efficiency, and establishing essential legal and governmental structures. His death, therefore, cast a long shadow, leaving the Caliphate grappling with questions of succession, administrative continuity, and preserving the fragile unity he had meticulously cultivated.

The process of selecting Umar(RA)'s successor was far from straightforward. Umar(RA), aware of the potential for conflict and instability, had attempted to establish a system for choosing his successor during his lifetime. He appointed a six-member council (Shura) to select the next Caliph. This council consisted of six prominent companions of the Prophet Muhammad(PBUH): `Ali(RA) ibn Abi Talib`, `Talha ibn Ubayd Allah`, `Zubayr ibn al-Awwam`, `Abd al-Rahman ibn Awf`, `Sa`d ibn Abi Waqqas`, and `Usman ibn Affan`. This committee's formation reflected Umar(RA)'s pragmatic approach to governance and his awareness of the potential for factionalism. By selecting figures of significant prestige and influence from different segments of the early Muslim community, Umar(RA) hoped to ensure a degree of consensus and stability during the transition.

However, the Shura's deliberations were not without their challenges. Despite their reverence for the Prophet and loyalty to Umar(RA), the council members held differing views regarding the most suitable candidate for the Caliphate. The intense and prolonged discussions highlighted the complexities of balancing political pragmatism with religious and personal considerations. This internal deliberation reflected the absence of a clear hereditary principle and the evolving nature of the political system within the early Islamic world.

The eventual selection of Uthman(RA) ibn Affan as Caliph was not unanimous, a fact that foreshadowed the difficulties that would plague his reign. Uthman(RA), a wealthy merchant and a close companion of the Prophet, possessed administrative experience and the personal piety considered essential for the role. However, his wealth and family connections to the Meccan elite raised concerns among some, who perceived a potential for bias and favouritism in his governance. His eventual selection after prolonged debate indicated the weight of the decision and the challenges in navigating the complex power dynamics within the nascent Caliphate.

The transition to Uthman(RA)'s rule was not without its immediate challenges. He inherited an empire that, while significantly expanded under Umar(RA), was still grappling with the complexities of administering a diverse and sprawling territory. The vast expanse of the conquered lands posed logistical challenges, from maintaining communications to ensuring efficient governance. Uthman(RA)'s administration faced the ongoing need to integrate conquered populations into the fabric of the Caliphate while maintaining order and resolving disputes. The sheer scale of the task placed immense pressure on the new Caliph.

Furthermore, Uthman(RA)'s leadership style differed from that of Umar(RA). While Umar(RA) was known for his austere lifestyle and direct engagement with the people, Uthman(RA), who came from a wealthy background, relied more heavily on established administrative channels and existing elite networks. This difference in style, though perhaps inevitable, led to criticism from segments of the population who believed that Uthman(RA) had become distant from the needs of the ordinary people. This perception and other grievances would fuel the growing discontent that ultimately contributed to the conflict that would engulf the Caliphate later in his reign.

Uthman(RA) faced significant financial challenges as well. The vast expansion of the Caliphate had necessitated substantial military expenditure. Managing the expanding Bayt al-Mal (the public treasury) required careful oversight, and the distribution of resources needed to be handled justly and fairly. In some cases, even if unfounded, allegations of favouritism further exacerbated the perception of a widening gap between the elite and the ordinary people. These financial concerns and governance-related grievances fuelled tensions and laid the groundwork for the subsequent conflicts.

The administrative structure of the Caliphate during Uthman(RA)'s reign inherited a system already developed under Abu Bakr(RA) and Umar(RA). However, the sheer scale of the empire and the need to maintain order among diverse populations necessitated a more structured and complex organisation. Uthman(RA) had to coordinate military campaigns, manage the vast public treasury, and resolve disputes in numerous regions simultaneously. This involved delegating authority to governors and officials across the empire, which carried risks of inefficiency and corruption.

Uthman(RA)'s reliance on his family and close associates in governance further fuelled existing tensions. While it is historically difficult to determine whether or not this was a deliberate policy of nepotism, the perceived bias in appointments exacerbated existing grievances among the populace. This perception of favouritism eroded public confidence in the leadership and exacerbated existing social and political divisions. It undermined Uthman(RA)'s attempts to maintain the unity and cohesion of the Caliphate, thereby contributing to the instability that would mark the later years of his reign.

One of the most significant challenges Uthman(RA) faced stemmed from his attempts to reconcile the expanding bureaucracy with the principles of early Islamic governance. This involved a delicate balancing act between consolidating power and maintaining the decentralisation that had defined the early years of the Caliphate. Uthman(RA)'s efforts to establish a more hierarchical administrative structure while improving efficiency also opened avenues for potential corruption and abuse of power. The balance between central control and local autonomy continued challenging governance within the Caliphate.

Therefore, the legacy of Umar(RA) ibn al-Khattab proved to be complex and multifaceted. While his death caused immediate concerns regarding succession, it also presented a crucial test to the mechanisms of power transition within the Caliphate. Umar(RA)'s administrative reforms and achievements shaped the foundations upon which Uthman(RA) built. However, the transition underscored the system's fragility and exposed inherent tensions within the rapidly expanding empire. The challenges Uthman(RA) faced immediately after assuming power served as a reminder that the consolidation of the Caliphate was not merely a matter of military success, but also one of navigating intricate internal dynamics and maintaining the delicate balance of power and justice within a diverse and sprawling empire. The seeds of future conflicts had already been sown, even as Uthman(RA) took up the mantle of leadership. The underlying issues of governance, social inequalities, and competing political factions were far from resolved. They would shape the turbulent years that lay ahead, ultimately leading to the First Fitna, a tragic period of civil war that shattered the early unity of the Islamic world.

Chapter 3: Uthman(RA) ibn Affan: Challenges and Controversies

Uthman(RA)'s Early Reign and Administrative Challenges

Uthman(RA) ibn Affan inherited a complex and volatile situation upon assuming the caliphate in 644 CE. The assassination of Umar(RA) ibn al-Khattab had shaken the foundations of the burgeoning Islamic empire, leaving a power vacuum and exposing deep-seated fissures within the Muslim community. While Umar(RA)'s reign had been marked by significant territorial expansion and administrative consolidation, it had also generated its challenges, many of which Uthman(RA) now had to confront. The immediate aftermath of Umar(RA)'s death was characterised by uncertainty and internal debate, as the six-member Shura grappled with selecting a successor. The choice of Uthman(RA), though ultimately decided, did not come without dissent, foreshadowing the difficulties that would mark his tenure.

One of Uthman(RA)'s most pressing challenges was the sheer scale and diversity of the empire he now governed.

Umar(RA)'s conquests had extended the Caliphate's reach across vast swathes of territory, encompassing diverse populations with varying cultural backgrounds and levels of integration into the Islamic political system. This created considerable logistical difficulties regarding communication, administration, and the equitable distribution of resources. The vast distances and diverse languages posed substantial hurdles to effective governance. Maintaining efficient communication networks alone was a monumental task, requiring establishing and maintaining well-functioning courier systems across deserts, mountains, and established trade routes. Uthman(RA)'s administration had to coordinate military deployments, collect taxes, dispense justice, and resolve conflicts in multiple regions simultaneously, requiring high organisation and efficiency.

The management of the Bayt al-Mal, the public treasury, became a focal point of concern during Uthman(RA)'s early reign. The considerable financial resources generated through taxation and tribute were crucial for sustaining the military, funding public works projects, and maintaining the administrative infrastructure. Effective resource allocation was vital for the stability and legitimacy of the Caliphate, and its mismanagement could have severe consequences. Uthman(RA) inherited a system that had undergone substantial development under Umar(RA), but the expanding empire required continuous refinement and adaptation. The allocation of funds for military expeditions, infrastructure projects, and social welfare programs had to be carefully managed to avoid exacerbating existing tensions.

Uthman(RA)'s administrative style differed significantly from that of Umar(RA). While Umar(RA) was known for his austere lifestyle and direct engagement with the populace, Uthman(RA), hailing from a wealthy Meccan family, adopted a more indirect approach. He often relied on established administrative channels and his existing network of advisors and officials. This was partly a consequence of the sheer scale of the empire, making it impossible for him to engage directly with all aspects of governance. However, this more distant approach contributed to a growing perception of detachment from the concerns of ordinary citizens. This perception, justified or not, fuelled discontent amongst segments of the population who felt alienated from the governing elite. Regardless of their accuracy, such perceptions played a crucial role in shaping political perceptions and fueling dissent. The difference in style is well documented in contemporary accounts, underscoring the challenges of maintaining legitimacy and popular support within such a diverse and extensive empire.

The early years of Uthman(RA)'s caliphate were also marked by attempts to consolidate and reform the existing administrative structures inherited from Umar(RA). This involved streamlining bureaucratic processes, enhancing the efficiency of tax collection, and establishing clearer communication channels across the empire. The empire's expansion meant a more formalised and structured administrative system capable of handling the increased workload and complexity of governance. Uthman(RA) appointed trusted officials in various regions, often relying on his established networks and family connections. While these appointments may have been based on merit and experience, the perception of nepotism, widespread among specific segments of the population, fueled discontent and added to the existing political tensions.

Furthermore, Uthman(RA) faced ongoing challenges stemming from the diverse religious and ethnic backgrounds within the empire. The integration of newly conquered populations into the political and social fabric of the Caliphate was a constant concern. Reconciling various legal traditions and cultural practices while maintaining the principles of Islamic governance was a delicate balancing act, requiring careful diplomacy and administrative skill. Maintaining internal security and suppressing any potential revolts or uprisings required vigilance and effective military deployments, all placing significant burdens on the already stretched resources of the administration. The success of this integration process was crucial to the long-term stability of the empire.

Therefore, the initial years of Uthman(RA)'s reign present a complex picture of challenges and achievements. He inherited an empire grappling with the consequences of rapid expansion and internal tensions. While he implemented administrative reforms aimed at streamlining governance and enhancing efficiency, these efforts were often met with criticism and accusations of favouritism, particularly amongst those segments of the population who felt marginalised or overlooked. The seeds of future conflicts were sown during these early years, as the growing discontent amongst certain groups within the Muslim community began to coalesce, eventually culminating in the events that would ultimately lead to the First Fitna and significantly alter the course of early Islamic history. Understanding Uthman(RA)'s early reign is essential to comprehending the ensuing turmoil and the complexities of the early Islamic political landscape. When coupled with deep-seated social and political divisions, the seemingly mundane challenges of administration and resource management ultimately played a crucial role in shaping the tumultuous years to come. The apparent success of the initial years should not overshadow the subtle yet significant tensions that characterised the period and ultimately proved detrimental to the Caliphate's long-term stability.

Economic Policies and Accusations of Favoritism

Uthman(RA) ibn Affan's economic policies, while arguably contributing to the material prosperity of the expanding Caliphate, became a significant source of contention and fueled the growing dissent that ultimately led to his assassination. His administration inherited a robust, albeit rapidly expanding, economic system established under Umar(RA) ibn al-Khattab. Umar(RA)'s policies, characterised by austerity and a focus on equitable resource distribution, laid the groundwork for a stable financial structure. However, the vast territorial gains under Umar(RA), particularly the conquests of Persia and Egypt, brought unprecedented wealth into the Bayt al-Mal, the public treasury. This sudden resource increase placed considerable strain on the existing administrative mechanisms and created new resource allocation and management challenges. Uthman(RA)'s approach to managing this burgeoning wealth differed significantly from that of his predecessor, laying the foundation for much of the criticism he faced.

One of the key criticisms against Uthman(RA) was his alleged favouritism in the distribution of state resources and the allocation of key governmental positions. Accusations of nepotism were widespread, particularly amongst those who felt excluded from the benefits of the empire's prosperity. While evidence suggests that Uthman(RA) did indeed favour members of his clan, the Banu Umayya, and close associates, determining the extent and nature of this favouritism requires carefully examining the available historical sources, which are often fragmented and biased. It is important to note that the concept of "nepotism," as understood in modern terms, may not fully capture the complexities of patronage networks in seventh-century Arabia. Uthman(RA)'s actions, often viewed through contemporary ethical standards, might have been viewed differently within the prevailing social and political context. However, the perception of favouritism, regardless of its reality, played a crucial role in fueling discontent and contributing to the growing political instability.

The distribution of land grants, a significant source of wealth and power in the early Islamic state, became a particularly contentious issue under Uthman(RA). Previous rulers had allocated land primarily based on military service and contribution to the state. However, under Uthman(RA), there were increasing reports of land grants awarded to his relatives and allies, regardless of their military or administrative contributions. These allegations fueled accusations that Uthman(RA) was enriching his clan while neglecting the needs of those who had fought for the Caliphate's expansion. The historical record reflects a complex picture, with some accounts supporting these allegations. In contrast, others offer alternative interpretations, suggesting that the land allocations were based on broader political and strategic considerations. However, the perception of injustice was potent enough to incite widespread resentment and anger.

Another area of concern was the allocation of positions of authority and influence within the administration. Critics pointed to the disproportionate number of Banu Umayya members appointed to crucial administrative and military roles. While Uthman(RA)'s supporters argued that these appointments were based on merit and competence, the critics countered that these choices reflected a prioritisation of kinship over ability, further exacerbating the perception of favouritism. The absence of a transparent meritocratic system in early Islamic administration meant that appointments were often influenced by personal connections and political allegiances, making such accusations difficult to refute conclusively. Many of these accounts rely on the testimony of opponents of Uthman(RA), making it crucial to approach these narratives with critical awareness. The lack of neutral, objective documentation presents significant challenges in verifying the true nature of these appointments.

The management of the Bayt al-Mal itself was subjected to intense scrutiny. While the treasury undeniably expanded significantly under Uthman(RA), the system lacked transparency and standardised record-keeping. This made it difficult to track the flow of resources and verify the fairness of their allocation. The absence of robust financial auditing mechanisms allowed accusations of mismanagement and misappropriation of funds to gain traction. Many accounts from the period describe lavish spending by Uthman(RA) and his associates, further contributing to the growing perception of inequality and corruption. Although some argue that Uthman(RA)'s spending was designed to cement alliances and maintain order in the expanding empire, the lack of transparency inevitably intensified the distrust among those who felt left out of the prosperity.

Beyond the accusations of nepotism, other economic policies also contributed to growing discontent. Although generally considered fair under Umar(RA), taxation practices changed under Uthman(RA)'s rule. Specific instances of tax increases or inequitable assessments, however localised, were quickly magnified and spread through rumours, leading to widespread resentment. Further fueling this discontent was the perceived inefficiency in distributing state resources to the provinces. While the empire's treasury overflowed, many provinces faced hardships, particularly those furthest from the centre of power in Medina. Regardless of its root causes, this discrepancy reinforced the perception of Uthman(RA)'s administration as being out of touch with the daily realities faced by many of the empire's citizens.

The growing dissatisfaction with Uthman(RA)'s economic policies did not immediately manifest as a unified or organised opposition movement. Initially, grievances were expressed through individual complaints and petitions. However, as the perception of injustice intensified, these scattered grievances coalesced, forming a larger opposition. This opposition, fueled by religious and political grievances, represented various social groups, including some of the early companions of the Prophet Muhammad(PBUH). The lack of clear channels for expressing dissent, coupled with the perceived insensitivity of Uthman(RA)'s administration, allowed opposition voices to gain greater resonance and influence. The culmination of these factors created a fertile ground for the escalation of conflict, setting the stage for the events that would forever mark the end of the Rashidun Caliphate and shape the future of early Islam.

In conclusion, the economic policies implemented under Uthman(RA) ibn Affan, while potentially fostering the material growth of the Caliphate, also created significant political challenges. The accusations of nepotism and favouritism, whether wholly accurate or partially exaggerated, undeniably contributed to widespread discontent. The lack of transparency in the management of the Bayt al-Mal, coupled with uneven distribution of resources and the perceived inefficiency of the administration, further exacerbated the situation. While Uthman(RA)'s actions might have been influenced by the time's prevailing social and political norms, the consequences were significant. The growing resentment created a powerful undercurrent of opposition, ultimately culminating in the events that led to the First Fitna and irrevocably altered the trajectory of the early Islamic state.

Analysing the economic factors and the resulting accusations helps to illuminate the complex interplay between political, financial, and social forces that shaped the tumultuous events of this pivotal era in Islamic history. It emphasises the importance of equitable governance and transparent administration, particularly within a rapidly expanding empire encompassing diverse populations and resources. The lessons from Uthman(RA)'s reign resonate today, highlighting the importance of economic justice and effective governance in ensuring political stability and social harmony.

The Growing Opposition and the Seeds of the First Fitna

The seeds of the First Fitna, the devastating civil war that shattered the unity of the Rashidun Caliphate, were sown long before the assassination of Uthman(RA) ibn Affan. While Uthman(RA)'s economic policies undoubtedly contributed to growing dissatisfaction, the opposition coalesced against him was far more complex than simple economic grievance. It stemmed from a confluence of factors: religious anxieties, political maneuvering, tribal loyalties, and personal ambitions, all simmering beneath the surface of the expanding empire.

One key element was the emergence of distinct factions within the Muslim community. The early Islamic community, initially unified by its shared faith and the leadership of the Prophet Muhammad(PBUH), gradually fragmented into various groups, each with its own interpretation of Islamic law and political aspirations. These factions, often based on tribal affiliations or differing interpretations of the Quran and Sunnah, competed for influence and power within the burgeoning state. The relatively centralised authority established under Abu Bakr(RA) and Umar(RA) began to fray under the strain of the Caliphate's rapid expansion. The growing distance between the central authority in Medina and the outlying provinces exacerbated these divisions, allowing regional grievances and independent power bases to flourish.

The growing power of the Banu Umayya, Uthman(RA)'s clan, became a significant source of resentment. While Uthman(RA)'s supporters pointed to their administrative capabilities and loyalty, critics perceived their influence as an affront to the ideals of equality and justice that supposedly underpinned the early Islamic state. This perception, whether accurate or not, fueled accusations of nepotism and fueled the opposition's narrative of an unjust and corrupt leadership. The concentration of wealth and power within a single clan clashed directly with the ideals of egalitarianism many associated with the early Islamic community. This perception, amplified by the lack of transparency in government, sowed deep seeds of mistrust and disaffection.

The grievances weren't solely confined to the elite. The ordinary citizens, particularly those in the provinces, also felt neglected. The rapid expansion of the empire stretched the administrative resources thin. Communication was difficult, and the central government's ability to address local concerns and grievances was limited. Many complained about the system's inefficiency, citing delays in the distribution of resources and the lack of responsiveness to their needs. This lack of responsiveness, combined with the rumours of lavish spending in Medina, further fueled the anger and resentment among the populace. The disconnect between the central government's prosperity and the average citizen's daily struggles created fertile ground for opposition.

Religious objections further complicated the political landscape. While the core tenets of Islam remained largely consistent, differing interpretations of the Quran and the Sunnah arose, leading to theological disputes and competing claims of religious authority. These interpretations often served as the basis for political and social divisions, adding another layer of complexity to the growing opposition against Uthman(RA). Certain groups viewed Uthman(RA)'s policies and actions as deviations from the true path of Islam, further bolstering their opposition. The use of religious justifications served to legitimise the growing rebellion, giving it a moral dimension that resonated powerfully with many members of the Muslim community.

The growing dissatisfaction eventually translated into overt expressions of dissent. Initially, these expressions were limited to petitions and complaints addressed to the Caliph, but as grievances mounted, they took a more confrontational turn. Delegations from various parts of the empire arrived in Medina, openly criticising Uthman(RA)'s policies and demanding reforms. These delegates represented a broad spectrum of the Muslim community, encompassing various tribes, social classes, and differing interpretations of Islamic doctrine. Their common ground was the deep discontent that had festered over time, amplified by the perceived injustices of Uthman(RA)'s rule.

The situation was further complicated by the emergence of influential figures who capitalised on the widespread discontent. These individuals, often charismatic and influential within their communities, skillfully exploited the growing resentment to advance their political ambitions. They expertly manipulated religious and tribal sentiments, weaving narratives that depicted Uthman(RA) as a tyrant who had betrayed the ideals of the early Islamic state. Their actions organised and focused the disparate opposition factions, transforming scattered grievances into a unified, increasingly powerful movement against Uthman(RA).

Uthman(RA)'s attempts at appeasement were largely unsuccessful. He attempted to address some of the grievances, but his efforts were often perceived as insufficient and insincere, given the deep-seated nature of the resentment against him. His efforts to appease the critics were usually seen as reactive rather than proactive, failing to address the root causes of the discontent. This reinforced the perception of Uthman(RA)'s detachment and incompetence, further fueling the growing opposition.

As the opposition grew in size and determination, the situation in Medina became increasingly volatile. The protests became more frequent and more insistent. The discontent gradually transformed into a full-blown political crisis, threatening to unravel the fabric of the Caliphate. The political climate became increasingly toxic, with rumours, accusations, and counter-accusations flying. The once-united community was now deeply divided, creating a dangerous environment for the fragile peace of the empire.

The final act played out tragically. The escalating tensions culminated in a siege of Uthman(RA)'s residence in Medina. The blockade, involving several armed opponents, lasted for several days. The Caliph, isolated and lacking sufficient support, was ultimately assassinated, bringing an abrupt and violent end to his reign. The assassination of Uthman(RA) marked not just the end of an era but the beginning of a period of unprecedented turmoil and bloodshed, the First Fitna, a civil war that would devastate the early Islamic world and irrevocably alter its course. The tragic events that unfolded revealed the profound fragility of the early Islamic state, highlighting the precarious balance between religious unity, political stability, and effective governance. The seeds of this conflict were sown in the complexities of an expanding empire, fueled by political rivalries, economic injustices, and contrasting interpretations of religious doctrine. The consequences would be far-reaching, extending for generations to come. The story of Uthman(RA)'s reign is a stark reminder of the challenges of governing a diverse population, balancing competing interests, and maintaining political stability amidst rapid societal change. The legacy of the First Fitna continues to resonate in the discussions on justice, governance, and political leadership within the Islamic world and beyond.

The Assassination of Uthman(RA) and its Immediate Aftermath

The assassination of Uthman(RA) ibn Affan in June 656 CE was not a sudden eruption of violence but the culmination of a long period of simmering discontent. While the immediate trigger might be debated amongst historians, the underlying causes were multifaceted and deeply rooted in the socio-political fabric of the expanding Islamic empire. The siege of his home in Medina lasted several days. It was not simply a spontaneous uprising but a meticulously planned operation involving a coalition of diverse groups united by their grievances against Uthman(RA)'s rule.

One prominent group involved was the faction of Medinan citizens who felt marginalised by Uthman(RA)'s perceived favouritism towards his clan, the Banu Umayya. Accusations of nepotism, of appointing family members to key administrative positions and granting them preferential treatment in the distribution of resources, fueled their resentment. This was not merely a matter of personal enrichment; it was perceived as a betrayal of the egalitarian ideals that had initially characterised the early Islamic community. These accusations, whether entirely accurate or exaggerated, tapped into a deep-seated anxiety about the concentration of power and wealth in the hands of a few. The lack of transparency in the Caliphate's financial dealings further amplified these concerns, fostering an atmosphere of mistrust and suspicion.

Adding to the pressure were the demands of the provinces. The rapid expansion of the Islamic empire during the reigns of Abu Bakr(RA) and Umar(RA) had strained administrative capabilities. The provinces, often distant from Medina, felt neglected and underrepresented. They complained about inadequate communication, delays in the distribution of resources, and a general lack of responsiveness from the central government. These grievances were compounded by economic hardships in certain regions, leading to a perception of injustice and inequality within the rapidly expanding empire. Delegations from Egypt, Iraq, and other provinces had arrived in Medina over the preceding years, voicing their complaints to Uthman(RA). While some of these grievances might have been addressed, the deep-seated feeling of neglect remained.

However, the opposition against Uthman(RA) wasn't solely fueled by economic grievances and administrative inefficiencies. Religious disputes and ideological differences played a pivotal role. Different interpretations of Islamic law and practices existed within the community, creating theological divides. Certain groups criticised Uthman(RA)'s governance as a deviation from the true path of Islam, adding a religious dimension to the political opposition. These interpretations were not merely academic but potent tools for mobilising political support and legitimising the movement against the Caliph. The opposition effectively presented itself as defenders of true Islamic principles against a corrupt and unjust leadership.

Tallha ibn Ubayd-Allah and Zubayr ibn al-Awwam, prominent figures among the early converts to Islam, initially hesitated to oppose Uthman(RA) openly. Both were companions of the Prophet Muhammad(PBUH) and commanded significant respect within the Muslim community. However, their initial reluctance eventually led to active participation in the opposition. They were instrumental in rallying support against Uthman(RA), leveraging their status and influence to attract diverse groups to the cause. Their involvement was crucial in transforming the scattered protests into a formidable movement.

The crucial role of those who ultimately carried out the assassination cannot be overlooked. While the precise details of who exactly delivered the fatal blows might remain debated, the leaders who mobilised and orchestrated the siege of Uthman(RA)'s residence bear considerable responsibility for the events that unfolded. These individuals skillfully manipulated existing grievances, employing religious rhetoric and highlighting perceived injustices to galvanise their supporters.

The assassination itself was chaotic. The siege of Uthman(RA)'s house was a protracted affair, marked by escalating tensions and sporadic clashes. Despite his attempts at negotiation and appeasement, Uthman(RA) remained isolated within his residence, his pleas for help ignored or unheeded. The lack of adequate military support from Medina's garrison further highlighted the extent of the opposition and the fragility of Uthman(RA)'s authority. This fact reinforces the perception of his failure to consolidate his support effectively.

The immediate aftermath of Uthman(RA)'s assassination was a period of extreme instability and uncertainty. The assassination itself did not resolve the underlying political and social tensions that had fueled the opposition. Instead, it unleashed a wave of chaos and violence. The city of Medina became a scene of turmoil, as different factions struggled for control. The death of the Caliph left a power vacuum, creating an environment ripe for contention and conflict.

The absence of a clear line of succession immediately following Uthman(RA)'s death created an open power struggle. While some called for Ali(RA) ibn Abi Talib, the Prophet Muhammad(PBUH)'s cousin and son-in-law, others continued to dissent, highlighting the deep divisions within the community. The initial response wasn't a unified grief or a call for immediate order, but a scramble for power and control.

The assassination did not quell the existing divisions within the Muslim community; it exacerbated them. The diverse groups that had opposed Uthman(RA), motivated by differing political ambitions, economic grievances, and theological disagreements, now found themselves in a position to assert their influence in the ensuing power vacuum. Following Uthman(RA)'s death, the period became a chaotic scramble for control, with different factions vying for power and authority. The early hopes of a swift resolution were quickly dashed as competing claims and interpretations regarding succession unfolded.

Different accounts suggest varying levels of responsibility for the assassination among the individuals involved, indicating the complex and decentralised nature of the opposition movement. Some accounts highlight the role of those directly involved in the violent act, emphasising their motives and the immediate consequences of their actions. Others focus on the individuals who mobilised support for the opposition, analysing their influence and the ideological currents they tapped into. This lack of a single, straightforward narrative is telling, underscoring the chaotic and multi-faceted nature of the event.

The immediate aftermath of Uthman(RA)'s death witnessed not just political instability but also a profound moral and religious crisis. The assassination of a Caliph, a leader chosen by the community to uphold Islamic law and order, challenged the very foundations of the early Islamic state. The act raised profound questions about the legitimacy of political authority and the principles of justice and governance within the rapidly expanding Islamic world. The assassination was not just a political event; it was a religious and moral shock to the early Muslim community.

The event was a turning point in the political history of the early Islamic empire and a critical moment in its intellectual and religious development. The ensuing debates and discussions surrounding the assassination of Uthman(RA) and the legitimacy of the subsequent leadership reflected the already growing tensions within the community regarding the interpretation of Islamic law and governance. The discussions surrounding these critical questions profoundly impacted the development of Islamic jurisprudence and political thought. The assassination of Uthman(RA), therefore, did not merely precipitate the First Fitna; it profoundly altered the course of Islamic history in ways that continue to be analysed and debated to this day. The legacy of this event serves as a cautionary tale, highlighting the challenges of maintaining unity and stability in the face of conflicting interests, growing ambitions, and fundamental disagreements regarding religious interpretations and political authority.

The Legacy of Uthman(RA) and the Transition to Ali(RA)

The death of Uthman(RA) ibn Affan left an undeniable mark on the nascent Islamic empire, a mark etched not just in blood but in the profound political and social divisions it exposed and exacerbated. His legacy remains a subject of intense scholarly debate, with historians grappling to reconcile his undeniable contributions to the consolidation of the nascent empire with the controversies that ultimately led to his demise. Uthman(RA)'s tenure as Caliph witnessed significant achievements. He oversaw the completion and standardisation of the Quranic text, a monumental task of immense religious and cultural importance that unified the burgeoning Muslim community under a single, authoritative scriptural source. This standardisation provided a crucial element of cohesion amidst the empire's rapid expansion, ensuring a consistent understanding and interpretation of the sacred text across diverse regions and communities. This achievement resonates powerfully throughout Islamic history, solidifying Uthman(RA)'s place as a significant figure in the development of Islamic scripture and religious practice.

Beyond the standardisation of the Quran, Uthman(RA)'s reign also saw the continuation of the remarkable military conquests that had characterised the previous caliphates. The expansion of the Islamic empire under his leadership pushed its borders further into Syria, Egypt, and Persia, cementing the status of Islam as a dominant force in the region. This expansion, however, also posed significant administrative challenges. Managing the vast and diverse territories under Islamic control required complex administrative systems and essential resources. Uthman(RA) attempted to address these challenges, initiating administrative reforms to improve efficiency and enhance communication between Medina and the provinces. However, his efforts were hampered by growing opposition, which frequently accused him of incompetence and bias.

The accusations of nepotism levelled against Uthman(RA) stemmed from his perceived preferential treatment of his Banu Umayya clan. Appointing family members to key administrative positions and granting them significant economic advantages fuelled resentment among the wider Muslim community. This perceived favouritism, whether based on factual evidence or fuelled by rumour and exaggeration, tapped into more profound anxieties surrounding the concentration of power and wealth within the empire. It contradicted the ideals of egalitarianism that had characterised the early Islamic community, leading to disillusionment and resentment among those who felt excluded from the benefits of the empire's expansion. The lack of transparency in the Caliphate's finances further exacerbated these concerns, contributing to a climate of mistrust and suspicion that ultimately contributed to his downfall.

Uthman(RA)'s attempts to address the economic grievances of the provinces were met with mixed success. The rapid expansion had strained resources and led to uneven distribution of wealth and opportunities. Some areas prospered, while others experienced hardship. The resulting discontent manifested as protests and accusations of neglect, adding pressure on Uthman(RA)'s authority. The lack of a robust and consistent system for taxation and resource allocation across the empire created additional challenges. This lack of responsiveness to the needs of the provinces was not just a matter of economic inefficiency; it became a powerful symbol of perceived injustice within the Muslim community, furthering the growing opposition to his leadership.

Beyond the economic and administrative issues, religious and ideological divisions played a significant role in shaping opposition to Uthman(RA). The early Islamic community was not monolithic in its spiritual understanding. Different schools of thought and interpretations of Islamic law coexisted, creating potential for theological disputes and political dissent. Some groups within the Muslim community criticised Uthman(RA)'s policies and governance as a deviation from true Islamic principles, framing their opposition not just as a political grievance but as a religious crusade. This intertwining of religious and political grievances further energised the opposition, providing a robust moral framework for their actions and attracting broader support.

The growing opposition to Uthman(RA) was not spontaneous; it was carefully organised and strategically mobilised. Key figures like Tallha ibn Ubayd-Allah and Zubayr ibn al-Awwam, prominent companions of the Prophet Muhammad(PBUH), initially hesitated to oppose Uthman(RA) openly. However, their eventual involvement proved crucial in galvanising support against the Caliph. Their established reputations and influence within the Muslim community helped unite diverse groups under a single banner of opposition, transforming isolated protests into a concerted challenge to Uthman(RA)'s authority. Their decision to join the opposition demonstrates the depth of the crisis and the erosion of faith in Uthman(RA)'s leadership among even those previously aligned with his authority.

The assassination of Uthman(RA) in 656 CE marked a turning point in early Islamic history. It was not just a violent event but a symptom of the deep-seated political, economic, and religious divisions within the Muslim community. The chaotic aftermath of his death highlighted the fragility of the nascent empire and the failure of its leadership to address the growing grievances of its diverse population effectively. The ensuing power vacuum created an environment ripe for contention and conflict, setting the stage for the First Fitna. This devastating civil war profoundly shaped the subsequent course of Islamic history.

The First Era of Islamic Leadership

Ali(RA) ibn Abi Talib, the Prophet Muhammad(PBUH)'s cousin and son-in-law, emerged as a prominent candidate to succeed Uthman(RA). His ascension, however, was far from seamless. He faced immediate challenges from the divisions and distrust sown during Uthman(RA)'s reign. While some within the Muslim community embraced Ali(RA)'s leadership as a return to the more egalitarian ideals of the early Islamic community, others remained deeply sceptical, pointing to the violence that had accompanied Uthman(RA)'s removal from power. This scepticism was exacerbated by Ali(RA)'s failure to immediately and decisively resolve the issues that had contributed to the growing discontent towards Uthman(RA)'s rule.

Ali(RA)'s attempts to address the inherited problems were met with significant resistance. The deep-seated divisions within the community made it difficult to implement practical solutions. The challenges were compounded by the lack of a unified vision among Ali(RA)'s supporters. His initial steps focused on attempting to consolidate his authority and address the immediate needs of the provinces. He tried to re-establish trust, address grievances, and reform the administrative structures that had grown dysfunctional under Uthman(RA). Yet, these efforts were complicated by factionalism and the lack of a single, unified support base. The deep-seated divisions within the community, fuelled by economic disparity, conflicting interpretations of Islamic law, and competing political ambitions, proved far more challenging to overcome than anticipated. The seeds of the First Fitna had already been sown, and Ali(RA)'s caliphate would be dominated by attempts to navigate these dangerous waters. His initial efforts to bring peace and stability to the empire would be tested, setting the scene for the escalating conflicts that would define the subsequent years and permanently alter the trajectory of early Islamic history. The legacy of Uthman(RA), therefore, is not solely his own, but is inextricably linked to the turbulent transition that followed, a transition that ultimately led to the First Fitna and a fundamentally altered Islamic world.

Chapter 3
Ali(RA) ibn Abi Talib: Leadership and the First Fitna

Ali(RA)'s Accession and the Challenges of Leadership

Ali(RA)'s accession to the caliphate in 656 CE was far from a triumphant coronation. The assassination of Uthman(RA) had left a gaping wound in the fabric of the nascent Islamic empire, a wound that festered with resentment, suspicion, and deeply entrenched political divisions. While Ali(RA) ibn Abi Talib, the Prophet Muhammad(PBUH)'s cousin and son-in-law, enjoyed widespread respect and held a position of undeniable authority within the community, his path to the caliphate was paved with obstacles, challenges that would ultimately define the early years of his reign and plunge the empire into the devastating First Fitna.

The immediate aftermath of Uthman(RA)'s death was characterised by chaos and uncertainty. Several influential figures within the Muslim community, including Talha ibn Ubayd-Allah and Zubayr ibn al-Awwam, both companions of the Prophet, initially refused to recognise Ali(RA)'s claim to the caliphate. Their reluctance stemmed not merely from personal ambition but also serious concerns about the legitimacy of Uthman(RA)'s removal and the potential for further violence. These concerns resonated throughout the community, dividing it into factions and creating a climate of distrust and instability. Ali(RA)'s ascension, therefore, was not a smooth transition of power but rather a precarious ascent to a position of leadership burdened by the unresolved issues of Uthman(RA)'s reign and the lingering anxieties surrounding the use of force in settling political disputes.

A significant segment of the Muslim community immediately questioned the legitimacy of Ali(RA)'s caliphate. Aisha, the Prophet's widow, along with Talha and Zubayr, openly challenged Ali(RA)'s authority, asserting that his acceptance of the caliphate was marred by the violence that had accompanied Uthman(RA)'s demise. They argued that a more peaceful and consensual process should have been followed, and that Ali(RA) failed to demonstrate the leadership qualities required to unite the fractured community. This challenge was not merely a personal feud; it represented a deeper ideological rift concerning the appropriate mechanisms for succession in the nascent Islamic state. The debate over legitimacy extended far beyond the individual ambitions of these key figures; it became a battle for the soul of the nascent Islamic state, a conflict that would shape the trajectory of the empire for decades to come. The initial challenges to Ali(RA)'s authority were not isolated incidents; they were symptomatic of a more profound crisis of leadership and governance.

Adding to Ali(RA)'s difficulties was the unresolved issue of Uthman(RA)'s assassination. While some rejoiced at Uthman(RA)'s death, viewing it as retribution for his alleged injustices, many others condemned the act as a violation of Islamic principles and a dangerous precedent for settling political disagreements. Ali(RA) faced immense pressure to bring the perpetrators to justice, but doing so risked alienating factions within the community who either supported Uthman(RA) or condoned the assassination. His failure to decisively and impartially address this issue exacerbated the existing divisions within the community, fueling further suspicion and distrust among his opponents. Navigating this delicate balance between justice and political expediency would prove to be one of the most significant challenges of Ali(RA)'s reign, a challenge that he would ultimately fail to overcome.

The administrative challenges inherited from Uthman(RA)'s reign compounded Ali(RA)'s political problems. The empire's vastness, the diversity of its populations, and the complexities of its administration demanded effective leadership, careful planning, and a unified vision. Uthman(RA)'s policies had been marred by accusations of nepotism and mismanagement, weakening the administrative structures and causing the provinces to experience economic hardship. Ali(RA)'s attempt to reform these structures was met with significant resistance, as various factions within the community were reluctant to surrender their positions of power and influence. These reforms were further hampered by the lack of a shared vision among Ali(RA)'s supporters, who remained fragmented and disorganised in their approach to governance.

Ali(RA)'s attempts to address the economic grievances of the provinces were equally challenging. The uneven distribution of wealth and the inefficient taxation system had created significant discontent, particularly in regions that felt neglected or marginalised by Uthman(RA)'s policies. Ali(RA)'s attempts to reform the system and ensure a more equitable distribution of resources required careful negotiation and decisive action. However, his efforts were undermined by the ongoing political crisis and the continuing resistance from powerful vested interests. The economic anxieties fueled by Uthman(RA)'s reign and the subsequent political instability created a vicious cycle, where economic hardship exacerbated political division and political turmoil further disrupted economic stability.

The theological and ideological differences within the Muslim community added another layer of complexity to Ali(RA)'s challenges. The early Islamic community was not monolithic, with different interpretations of Islamic law and divergent approaches to governance coexisting. These differences, often overlooked or suppressed during the earlier caliphates, intensified after Uthman(RA)'s death, causing deeper rifts within the community. Ali(RA) attempted to address these differences through dialogue and diplomacy, but the level of mistrust and the strength of the various ideological factions made reconciliation incredibly difficult. The lack of a clear and universally accepted interpretation of Islamic law exacerbated the political division, turning theological disagreements into powerful catalysts for conflict.

The situation in the provinces further complicated Ali(RA)'s position. The vast empire, newly acquired through rapid military conquests, required competent governors and an effective communication system. Uthman(RA)'s appointments, often criticised for favouritism, had left some regions resentful and others poorly managed. Ali(RA) faced the daunting task of replacing corrupt or ineffective governors, while at the same time avoiding alienating those who were loyal to Uthman(RA) or his policies. Balancing the competing demands of different regions and accommodating the diverse opinions within the empire became a nearly impossible task, requiring a degree of political skill and diplomacy that exceeded even his considerable capabilities.

In addition to the internal challenges, Ali(RA) faced external threats. The Byzantine Empire remained a powerful rival, and the Sasanian Persian Empire, though weakened by recent conflicts, still posed a threat in the east. These external pressures strained the empire's resources. They diverted attention from urgent internal problems, forcing Ali(RA) to balance the need for internal stability with the imperative of maintaining the security of the empire's borders. Managing internal and external threats simultaneously proved overwhelming, further contributing to the growing crisis. These internal and external pressures created a perfect storm that would inevitably lead to open conflict and the disastrous First Fitna.

Ali(RA)'s efforts to consolidate his power and establish a stable governance were constantly undermined by the deep-seated divisions within the community. His attempts at reconciliation were frequently met with hostility and distrust, and his attempts to impose order were met with resistance from powerful factions who sought to exploit the existing divisions for their political ends. The lack of a unified vision and the persistence of political factions meant that setbacks in one area often undid any progress achieved in another. The seeds of the First Fitna were sown long before Ali(RA) acceded to the caliphate, but his reign would become the crucible in which these conflicts would boil over into open warfare. His reign is a stark reminder of the immense challenges faced by those attempting to build a cohesive and equitable society in the face of profound political, economic, and ideological divisions. The story of Ali(RA)'s leadership during this turbulent period is not just a historical narrative; it is a cautionary tale about the fragility of power and the difficulty of forging unity from deep-seated divisions.

The Battle of Siffin and its Aftermath

The escalating tensions between Ali(RA) and his opponents, Aisha, Talha, and Zubayr, finally culminated in the Battle of Jamal in 656 CE. While Ali(RA) emerged victorious, the conflict further fractured the Muslim community, leaving deep wounds that would not easily heal. Though militarily decisive for Ali(RA), the battle did little to resolve the underlying political and ideological disagreements that fueled the First Fitna. Instead, it hardened positions and created new enemies, setting the stage for the even more consequential Battle of Siffin.

The Battle of Siffin, fought in 657 CE near the Euphrates River, pitted Ali(RA)'s forces against the army of Muawiya ibn Abi Sufyan, the governor of Syria. Muawiya, a powerful and shrewd politician, had refused to recognise Ali(RA)'s caliphate, demanding retribution for Uthman(RA)'s assassination. He skillfully used the unresolved issue of Uthman(RA)'s death to rally support, exploiting the deep-seated grievances and suspicions that permeated the Muslim community. Muawiya's strategic brilliance lay not just in his military capabilities but in his masterful manipulation of the political landscape, adeptly exploiting existing divisions for his gain. His campaign was built on military strength and a shrewd understanding of the political currents and deep-seated grievances that roiled the Muslim world.

The armies at Siffin were considerable. Ali(RA)'s forces, while numerically superior, were a heterogeneous collection of diverse groups, reflecting the divisions within the community. Some genuinely believed in Ali(RA)'s legitimacy and fought for his leadership; others joined with reservations or ulterior motives, their loyalties fragile and easily swayed. The internal divisions within Ali(RA)'s army had a significant impact on their battle tactics. Lack of unified command, conflicting loyalties, and diverse interpretations of warfare significantly diminished their battlefield effectiveness. Therefore, the very composition of his army presented a significant challenge to effective military strategy.

Muawiya's army, though smaller, was better organised and more unified. He had spent considerable time consolidating his support in Syria, creating a cohesive fighting force loyal to his cause. This unity of purpose translated into a more disciplined and effective military machine on the battlefield. Moreover, Muawiya's astute political maneuvering had ensured a relatively high morale amongst his troops, making them formidable opponents. His army's transparent chain of command contributed to their effectiveness, allowing for coordinated tactics and improved battlefield performance.

The battle itself was protracted and brutal. It lasted for several days, characterised by fierce fighting and heavy casualties on both sides. Intense cavalry charges, desperate hand-to-hand combat, and the relentless exchange of projectiles characterised the fighting. Both armies displayed remarkable courage and resilience, illustrating the deep-seated passions fueling the conflict. Accounts of the battle suggest intense desperation, showcasing both sides' commitment to their cause.

A crucial moment arrived when Muawiya's troops raised copies of the Quran on their lances, invoking the divine word to settle their differences. This clever tactical maneuver exploited the religious sensibilities of many within Ali(RA)'s army, causing internal dissent and weakening their resolve. This religious appeal, however, was not a genuine attempt at peaceful resolution but rather a tactical ploy aimed at dismantling Ali(RA)'s coalition. It exposed the precariousness of Ali(RA)'s command, highlighting the divisions within his ranks that were waiting for an opportunity to exploit the lack of unity within the army.

Ali(RA), faced with the moral dilemma of continuing the battle against troops invoking the Quran, reluctantly agreed to arbitration. This decision, intended to prevent further bloodshed and find a peaceful solution, would be a catastrophic miscalculation. Arbitration, a process designed to resolve conflict peacefully, exacerbated existing divisions and sowed the seeds of even greater conflict.

The arbiters chosen, Amr ibn al-As for Muawiya and Abu Musa al-Ash'ari for Ali(RA), failed to deliver a just or acceptable outcome. Political maneuvering, personal ambitions, and a lack of impartiality clouded their deliberations. Amr ibn al-As, a skilled strategist and political operator, played his role masterfully, using his sharp wit and negotiating tactics to manipulate the arbitration process to his advantage. Abu Musa al-Ash'ari, known for his religious piety but lacking the necessary political acumen, was no match for Amr's diplomatic prowess.

The outcome of the arbitration was a deadlock, effectively leaving the question of the caliphate unresolved. Abu Musa, hoping to restore some semblance of harmony, attempted to annul Ali(RA)'s and Muawiya's claims, proposing a return to a less rigidly defined system of governance. Amr, however, cleverly outmaneuvered him, using the opportunity to declare Muawiya the caliph, thus effectively ending any possibility of a peaceful resolution. This decision irrevocably fractured the Muslim community, creating profound animosity and deepening the already significant divisions within Islam.

The arbitration's outcome led to a mass exodus of Ali(RA)'s supporters, many of whom felt betrayed by his decision to arbitrate and disappointed by the result. These individuals, known as the Kharijites, rejected Ali(RA) and Muawiya, arguing that the true path to Islamic governance lay outside the established system. They rejected the authority of both Ali(RA) and Muawiya, arguing that divine appointment, rather than political processes, should choose the rightful leader, and they felt that both leaders had compromised their faith through the arbitration.

The Kharijites' rejection of both Ali(RA) and Muawiya was a significant development. They represented a radical fringe group, but their emergence signalled a profound shift in the political landscape. Their beliefs, emphasising the direct application of Islamic law and the rejection of compromise, would significantly impact the later course of Islamic history. This rejection underscored the depth of the ideological and political divisions within the Muslim community that went far beyond the specific events of Siffin and the arbitration.

The aftermath of Siffin and the arbitration was a period of deepening political instability. The Muslim community, already fractured by years of conflict, was now irrevocably divided. The trust and unity that had characterised the early years of the Islamic state were shattered, making the reunification of the community an impossible task. Ali(RA)'s authority was significantly weakened, and his support was eroded by the arbitration's result and the departure of many supporters. Muawiya's position, however, was strengthened considerably, giving him a significant advantage in the ensuing power struggle.

The Battle of Siffin and its aftermath mark a turning point in early Islamic history. It highlighted the failure of the established political system and revealed the deep-seated ideological and political divisions that had been simmering beneath the surface for years. The conflict exposed the fragility of unity within the community and the potentially disastrous consequences of unresolved political disputes. The outcome of Siffin set the stage for further conflict. It ultimately signalled the end of the Rashidun Caliphate, ushering in an era of prolonged civil war and profound transformation within the Islamic world. The legacy of Siffin remains etched in Islamic history, a reminder of the enduring challenges of governing a diverse and dynamic society during a time of profound upheaval. The consequences of this battle would echo through generations, shaping the trajectory of the Islamic empire and leaving an indelible mark on the history of the early Muslim community.

The Kharijites and the Challenges toAlis Authority

The departure of those who rejected Ali(RA) and Muawiya following the disastrous arbitration at Siffin marked a pivotal moment in the early history of Islam. These dissidents, known as the Kharijites, represented a significant challenge to Ali(RA)'s authority and a profound fracturing of the nascent Muslim community. Their emergence wasn't simply a reaction to a specific event; it reflected more profound ideological disagreements and a growing dissatisfaction with the established political order. The Kharijites' rejection wasn't merely a political maneuver; it represented a fundamental divergence in understanding the principles of Islamic governance and leadership. Their beliefs, practices, and actions fundamentally reshaped the political landscape of the time and left an enduring legacy on Islamic thought and practice.

The Kharijites' core ideology centred on the concept of *al-hukm*, meaning "rulership" or "judgment." They believed that leadership in the Muslim community should be solely based on piety and adherence to the Quran and Sunnah (the Prophet Muhammad(PBUH)'s teachings and practices), without consideration for tribal affiliations, political expediency, or personal ambition. This radical principle differed sharply from the prevailing understanding of leadership, which often incorporated elements of tribal consensus and political pragmatism. The Kharijites argued that any leader who compromised Islamic principles, regardless of their past actions or piety, was illegitimate. This starkly contrasts with the prevalent view, where past deeds and alliances often played a significant role in assessing a leader's suitability. This principle of strict adherence to religious tenets made them fiercely critical of those they saw as compromising Islamic law.

Their rejection of arbitration itself demonstrated this principle. They saw the arbitration process as a violation of Islamic law, a compromise of the religious tenets, and a betrayal of God's will. To them, resorting to arbitration instead of continuing the jihad (holy war) against those deemed infidels represented a compromise on Islamic ideals, rendering Ali(RA)'s leadership illegitimate. They viewed the arbitration not as a means to resolve conflict, but as a concession to worldly power, prioritising political expediency over religious rectitude. This perception played a crucial role in their alienation from the mainstream of the Muslim community and hardening their belief in the necessity of establishing an alternative, more strictly adherent system of governance.

This uncompromising stance led them to challenge the authority of both Ali(RA) and Muawiya. They saw Ali(RA)'s agreement to arbitration as an act of weakness and a deviation from the true path of Islam, and they held Muawiya responsible for exploiting the situation to seize power through illegitimate means. Both leaders, in their eyes, had compromised their religious obligations for worldly gain. This led the Kharijites to view both Ali(RA) and Muawiya as equally illegitimate, furthering the fragmentation of the Muslim community. Their rejection was not a simple matter of choosing sides in a power struggle, but a profound theological objection to the principles underlying Ali(RA)'s and Muawiya's leadership.

The Kharijites weren't a monolithic group, and internal divisions emerged within their ranks. Different factions arose, each with their interpretations of Islamic law and leadership. Some advocated a strict interpretation of *taqlid* (following precedent), while others emphasised *ijtihad* (independent reasoning in Islamic jurisprudence). These variations reflected the intellectual vibrancy and diversity within the movement, highlighting the breadth and complexity of the early Islamic debates surrounding religious and political authority. These internal disagreements, however, did not negate their unified rejection of Ali(RA) and Muawiya or their distinct theological beliefs, which provided a foundation for their unique interpretation of religious and political authority.

Their opposition manifested not only in theological debate but also in military action. Several significant battles and uprisings marked their challenge to the established power structures. These revolts often involved a combination of ideological zeal and pragmatic political calculations. Their military actions often involved guerrilla warfare tactics, leveraging the advantages of their intimate knowledge of local terrain, enabling them to resist larger, more conventional armies. This reflects a military strategy that was strategically adapted to their specific circumstances and aimed to exploit vulnerabilities in the larger established armies of both Ali(RA) and Muawiya.

The Kharijites' military activities, although often unsuccessful in terms of establishing their long-term political dominance, significantly destabilised the region. Though usually sporadic, their attacks significantly undermined Ali(RA)'s and Muawiya's authority, weakening both leaders' ability to govern the rapidly expanding Muslim Empire effectively. By perpetually challenging the established power structures, they contributed to a prolonged period of instability and violence, further contributing to the fragmentation of the Muslim community. Their continual uprisings diverted resources and manpower, diverting crucial attention and resources away from both leaders' ambitions of consolidating power and restoring unity. The persistent threat posed by the Kharijites' rebellious activities effectively prevented any lasting stability from emerging during this period.

The impact of the Kharijites extended far beyond their military actions. Their uncompromising ideology and insistence on strict adherence to Islamic principles profoundly influenced subsequent theological and political developments. Their rejection of compromise and emphasis on the direct application of the Quran and Sunnah became a hallmark of their movement. This emphasis on the fundamental principles of Islam served as a constant reminder to the established authorities of the ongoing need for strict religious adherence in governance. The very existence of this radical group shaped the political climate, leading to changes in governance strategies and the careful consideration of religious implications in political actions.

Despite failing to establish a lasting political entity, the Kharijites played a crucial role in shaping early Islam's intellectual and theological landscape. Their rigorous interpretation of Islamic law and emphasis on *tawheed* (the absolute oneness of God) influenced later schools of Islamic thought. Their legacy is evident in the subsequent development of various legal and theological schools, which grappled with the issues raised by the Kharijites' challenges. The Kharijites are remembered not only for their military actions but also for their lasting contribution to theological debates, demonstrating how their theological contributions profoundly altered the broader course of Islamic thought.

Their legacy serves as a testament to the complexities of early Islamic history. They exemplify the ongoing struggle between religious ideals and political realities, highlighting the tensions between strict adherence to religious principles and the pragmatic compromises often necessary in governance. The Kharijites' story underscores the profound internal divisions within the early Muslim community, revealing the difficulties faced in forging a cohesive identity in rapidly changing circumstances and demonstrating how theological disagreements could profoundly impact the political landscape. Their challenge to authority continues to resonate in the study of early Islamic history, reminding us of the enduring relevance of their theological and political contributions. Their legacy remains a significant part of the broader narrative of the formative years of Islam, influencing both religious and political discourse for centuries to come. Their story thus serves as a vital lens through which to study the complexities of early Islamic history and the ongoing struggle between religious ideals and political realities.

The Battle of Nahrawan and the Suppression of the Kharijites

The simmering discontent among the Kharijites, fueled by their rejection of arbitration and Ali(RA)'s perceived compromise, culminated in open rebellion. Their scattered bands, initially operating through guerrilla tactics and hit-and-run attacks, began to coalesce into a more organised force, posing a significant threat to Ali(RA)'s authority. This burgeoning threat necessitated a decisive confrontation, a confrontation that would take place at Nahrawan, a strategically important location near modern-day Baghdad. The Battle of Nahrawan, fought in 658 CE, remains a pivotal event in early Islamic history, marking a brutal chapter in the First Fitna and profoundly impacting the future trajectory of the nascent Islamic empire.

Despite their ideological unity in rejecting Ali(RA) and Muawiya, the Kharijites lacked a centralised command structure. Various groups, operating independently, added to the challenge of suppressing the rebellion. This decentralised nature, while making them difficult to defeat definitively, also made it difficult to coordinate their efforts effectively. Ali(RA)'s forces, though numerically superior, faced the difficult task of engaging a dispersed enemy adept at utilising unconventional warfare tactics. The Kharijites were not simply a disorganised rabble; their commitment to their cause, fueled by their unwavering belief in their interpretation of Islamic principles, manifested in a ferocious resistance against Ali(RA)'s army.

The battle itself was characterised by intense fighting. Ali(RA)'s army, a blend of experienced veterans and newly recruited soldiers, employed more conventional military strategies. They used their numerical advantage and superior training to overwhelm the Kharijite positions. Still, the Kharijites' knowledge of the terrain and determination enabled them to withstand the initial onslaught. The battle was not a straightforward victory for Ali(RA); it was a hard-fought struggle involving large-scale engagements and more minor, localised skirmishes. This highlights the fluid and dynamic nature of the conflict, illustrating the challenges Ali(RA)'s army faced against an enemy that expertly adapted to changing circumstances.

Accounts of the battle vary, highlighting the inherent difficulties in reconstructing a conflict over thirteen centuries ago. Sources differ on the exact number of combatants, casualties, and the precise sequence of events, contributing to the enduring complexities surrounding interpreting the conflict. Different historical narratives emphasise varying aspects of the battle, highlighting different interpretations of the actions and motivations of both sides. This discrepancy in historical accounts is a constant reminder that studying any historical event requires a meticulous and nuanced approach, necessitating the incorporation of multiple perspectives to generate a fuller and more balanced understanding.

The aftermath of Nahrawan was marked by significant bloodshed. The Kharijites suffered heavy losses, although the exact figures remain debated by historians. Ali(RA)'s victory, however, came at a substantial cost, both militarily and politically. The battle resulted in a devastating loss of life among the Kharijites, many of whom were executed after their capture. This harsh response, although possibly necessary from Ali(RA)'s perspective to quell the rebellion, fueled further resentment and ultimately contributed to the ongoing instability of the time. Moreover, the brutality of the battle further entrenched the divisions within the Muslim community.

The ethical implications of the Battle of Nahrawan remain a subject of considerable debate among Islamic scholars and historians. Some argue that Ali(RA)'s actions were justified as a necessary measure to maintain order and suppress a violent rebellion that threatened to undermine the unity of the nascent Islamic state. They highlight the threat posed by the Kharijites' actions, emphasising that Ali(RA)'s decision was a pragmatic necessity to maintain peace and stability. This perspective tends to view the battle in the broader context of early Islamic governance, arguing that Ali(RA)'s primary concern was preserving the larger society.

Others criticise Ali(RA)'s harsh treatment of the Kharijites, arguing that his actions violated Islamic principles of compassion and forgiveness. They point to the significant number of Kharijites killed after their surrender as evidence of a disregard for human life, a contrast to the ideals of mercy and justice emphasised in the Islamic faith. This perspective focuses on the ethical dilemmas of violent conflict, challenging the idea that any political objective justifies the violation of fundamental moral principles. The debate about the ethics of the Battle of Nahrawan underscores the ongoing complexities inherent in evaluating historical events within a moral and religious framework.

The Battle of Nahrawan had lasting political consequences regardless of the ethical interpretations. While it temporarily suppressed the Kharijite rebellion, it failed to eliminate the ideological threat. The movement, although weakened, continued to operate underground, launching further sporadic uprisings throughout the region. This highlights the limitations of military solutions to ideological conflicts, demonstrating how even a decisive military victory did not necessarily resolve the underlying ideological differences fueling the rebellion. The enduring impact of the Kharijites on Islamic history is shown by their continued persistence, even after suffering a considerable defeat at Nahrawan.

The battle also impacted Ali(RA)'s standing within the Muslim community. While the suppression of the Kharijites might have seemed like a strategic victory, the violence generated by the battle alienated some who disapproved of his methods. The actions of Ali(RA) at Nahrawan resulted in a variety of interpretations, furthering the divisions within the Muslim community. Some viewed it as a decisive victory against a dangerous threat, others saw it as a display of excessive brutality, and others saw it as a sign of weakening authority among the established leaders. These diverse interpretations indicate the complexities and nuances in reactions to the conflict, which had lasting effects on the early Islamic society and further fractured the delicate political unity of the fledgling empire.

The Battle of Nahrawan, therefore, serves as a complex case study in early Islamic history. It reveals the fragility of the newly established caliphate, the internal tensions within the Muslim community, and the multifaceted nature of the First Fitna. The battle was a military encounter, a clash of ideologies, a struggle for power, and a critical moment in shaping early Islamic political and religious thought. The enduring legacy of the battle lies not only in its military consequences but also in its continued impact on theological debate and the long-term political stability of the Islamic world. The ongoing debates surrounding the ethics and consequences of this conflict testify to its continuing relevance as a critical event shaping the development of Islamic history. Its complex nature highlights the enduring challenges in interpreting events with many perspectives and consequences, both immediate and long-lasting. The significance of Nahrawan continues to resonate in the study of early Islamic history, offering a rich and multifaceted lens for understanding the complexities of a pivotal era.

The Assassination of Ali(RA) and the End of the Rashidun Caliphate

The aftermath of Nahrawan, while seemingly solidifying Ali(RA)'s position, ultimately proved a pyrrhic victory. The brutal suppression of the Kharijites, though temporarily effective in quelling their immediate threat, further fractured the already fragile unity of the Muslim community. The accusations of excessive violence against surrendered fighters cast a long shadow, fueling resentment and undermining Ali(RA)'s credibility amongst those who valued Islamic principles of mercy and justice. This internal discord created a fertile ground for the machinations of Ali(RA)'s opponents, most notably Muawiya, the governor of Syria.

Muawiya, possessing considerable political acumen and a strong military base in Syria, had consistently challenged Ali(RA)'s authority. He skillfully leveraged the simmering discontent within the Muslim world to his advantage. The lingering disputes over the arbitration at Siffin and the unresolved issues surrounding Uthman(RA)'s assassination provided fertile ground for Muawiya's campaign to discredit Ali(RA) and consolidate his power. He cleverly employed propaganda, skillfully portraying himself as the champion of justice and order, seeking retribution for Uthman(RA)'s death, a narrative that resonated with a significant portion of the Muslim population. Muawiya's systematic and calculated denigration of Ali(RA) further eroded the latter's support base. He systematically portrayed Ali(RA)'s victory at Nahrawan not as a righteous action but as a bloodbath, alienating many Muslims who had reservations about Ali(RA)'s increasingly authoritarian actions.

The escalating tension between Ali(RA) and Muawiya created a perilous situation for the caliphate. The political landscape was deeply divided, with the Muslim community split along lines of allegiance to either Ali(RA) or Muawiya. This polarisation effectively paralysed the caliphate's ability to address other pressing issues, from administrative challenges to the continued threat of external enemies. The division within the ranks of the Muslim leadership became an existential threat to the very survival of the nascent empire. The potential for further conflict grew exponentially, placing the fragile peace and stability painstakingly established by the first three caliphs in severe jeopardy.

The divisions deepened, fuelled by religious as well as political differences. The Kharijites, though weakened by their defeat at Nahrawan, continued to represent a significant ideological threat. Their radical interpretation of Islam, emphasising strict adherence to religious principles and rejection of any perceived compromises, posed a constant source of unrest and dissent. The inability of Ali(RA) to reconcile these differences only served to embolden his opponents further and exacerbate the internal divisions within the Muslim community.

Within this volatile political environment, the assassination of Ali(RA) in 661 CE marked a tragic culmination of the First Fitna. The circumstances surrounding his death remain shrouded in some historical ambiguity, with different accounts highlighting different facets of the event. However, it is generally accepted that Abd-al-Rahman ibn Muljam, a Kharijite, assassinated Ali(RA) during the Fajr prayer in Kufa. This act of violence, while seemingly an individual act of extremism, was a culmination of the deep-seated political and religious divisions that had plagued the caliphate during Ali(RA)'s reign.

The assassination of Ali(RA) had profound and lasting consequences. The death of the fourth Rashidun Caliph effectively marked the end of the era of the Rightly Guided Caliphs. The subsequent power struggle and succession crisis precipitated prolonged instability and conflict within the Muslim world. Ali(RA)'s demise left a gaping power vacuum, exacerbating the already significant political divisions within the empire.

The immediate aftermath was characterised by further turmoil and violence. Ali(RA)'s death created a chaotic succession struggle between his supporters and the supporters of Muawiya. Ali(RA)'s son, Hasan, briefly assumed the caliphate, but his reign was short-lived. Facing overwhelming opposition from Muawiya's forces and recognising the devastating consequences of further civil war, Hasan ultimately ceded power to Muawiya in 661 CE. This agreement, however, did not resolve the underlying issues and only served as a reprieve from the escalating conflict. It represented a devastating blow to the supporters of Ali(RA), effectively marking the end of the Rashidun Caliphate and ushering in the Umayyad era.

The transition to the Umayyad Caliphate was far from smooth. While Muawiya's ascension brought stability after the tumultuous period of the First Fitna, it did so at a significant cost. The deep divisions within the Muslim community remained unresolved. The years of conflict and the lingering resentment over Ali(RA)'s death and Hasan's surrender sowed the seeds of future dissent and rebellion. The legacy of the First Fitna continued to shape the political landscape of the Islamic world for generations to come.

The death of Ali(RA), however, is more than simply a marker of the end of a political era. It represented a turning point in the evolution of Islamic governance and political thought. The assassination itself and the subsequent succession crisis highlighted the inherent fragility of the early Islamic state, the immense challenge of reconciling divergent interpretations of Islamic principles, and the limitations of relying solely on military solutions to resolve deeply rooted political and religious conflicts. The subsequent Umayyad Caliphate, though achieving a degree of stability, departed significantly from the ideals of the Rashidun era, demonstrating the irreversible consequences of the internal struggles that defined the First Fitna.

The First Era of Islamic Leadership

The legacy of the First Fitna extends beyond the political realm. The theological and ideological ramifications were profound and long-lasting. The differences in interpretations of Islamic law and practice that emerged during this period led to distinct theological schools of thought, shaping the course of Islamic jurisprudence and theology for centuries to come. The debates surrounding the legitimacy of Ali(RA)'s caliphate, the role of arbitration, and the ethical implications of violence in pursuing political goals continued to shape Islamic intellectual discourse. This ongoing debate reflects the multifaceted nature of the First Fitna, its complex legacy reaching far beyond the immediate political upheaval of the 7th century.

The assassination of Ali(RA) and the end of the Rashidun Caliphate thus serve as a powerful case study in the complexities of early Islamic history. It highlights the interplay of religious fervour, political ambition, and military power in shaping the early Islamic world. The enduring impact of this period is evident in the continued debates surrounding its events and interpretations, underscoring its significance in understanding the foundational elements of Islamic civilisation and the challenges confronting the newly established state in its formative years. The study of the First Fitna remains crucial for comprehending the immediate historical context and the enduring implications for the subsequent development of Islamic political and religious thought. Its legacy is woven into the fabric of Islamic history, a constant reminder of the fragility of unity and the lasting consequences of internal divisions in a society striving to define its identity and future.

Chapter 4
The First Fitna: A Civil War that Shattered the Unity of the Caliphate

The Causes of the First Fitna A Deep Dive into Political and Religious Divisions

The seeds of the First Fitna were sown long before Ali(RA)'s assassination. While broadly accepted, the seamless succession from the Prophet Muhammad(PBUH) to Abu Bakr(RA) masked underlying tensions and simmering disagreements that would eventually erupt into open warfare. The very nature of the caliphate itself, a novel political structure born from the unique circumstances of the Prophet's death, lacked a clearly defined framework for succession, leaving the door open to competing claims and interpretations. While the first three caliphs – Abu Bakr(RA), Umar(RA), and Uthman(RA) – enjoyed periods of relative stability, their reigns were not without their challenges, which contributed significantly to the fracturing of the Muslim community.

The Ridda Wars, undertaken by Abu Bakr(RA) to quell rebellions in the Arabian Peninsula immediately after the Prophet's death, exposed the fragility of the newly established Islamic state and revealed the deeply ingrained tribal loyalties that often superseded religious allegiance. The successful subjugation of these rebellions, though a testament to the military prowess of the nascent caliphate, also highlighted the brutality sometimes necessary to maintain control and consolidated the power of the central leadership. This inevitably led to resentment in certain quarters, especially amongst those who felt their interests were overlooked in consolidating power. The subsequent expansion under Umar(RA), though undeniably successful in territorial gains, also expanded the administrative challenges, further stressing the system and creating opportunities for dissent.

The reign of Uthman(RA), the third caliph, proved particularly tumultuous. Accusations of nepotism and favouritism towards his clan, the Umayyad, fueled widespread discontent. His administrative policies, including the appointment of governors and the distribution of resources, alienated significant portions of the Muslim population. Whether entirely accurate or exaggerated by his opponents, these accusations tapped into existing grievances and deep-seated tribal rivalries within the community. The concentration of power and wealth within certain clans, primarily fueled by the spoils of war, fostered resentment amongst others who felt marginalised and excluded from the benefits of the expanding empire. This contributed to the growing sense of injustice and fueled the calls for reform and accountability.

The assassination of Uthman(RA) in 656 CE marked a pivotal turning point. While the immediate cause may have been the culmination of years of simmering discontent, the event acted as a catalyst, shattering the fragile unity of the caliphate and unleashing the forces of conflict that would engulf the Muslim world for years to come. The assassination triggered a complex chain reaction, exposing deep religious and political divisions that had long been suppressed. The act was a stark demonstration of the breakdown in societal order and the failure of the existing political system to address fundamental grievances and conflicts. The ensuing power struggle to succeed Uthman(RA) immediately triggered the First Fitna.

The issue of succession to the caliphate was inherently complex. There was no divinely ordained mechanism for determining the rightful successor. Electing a caliph through consultation (shura) had proven effective in the past, but it also contained the seeds of its destruction. The lack of clear rules and guidelines created an environment ripe for competing claims, accusations of illegitimacy, and using power to secure political advantage. The subsequent struggle between Ali(RA) and Muawiya, each claiming legitimacy based on differing interpretations of Islamic principles and political expediency, directly reflected these inherent flaws.

Ali(RA)'s claim to the caliphate, based partly on his close kinship with the Prophet and perceived superior piety, faced strong opposition. Muawiya, governor of Syria, refused to recognise Ali(RA)'s authority, demanding retribution for Uthman(RA)'s assassination. Though seemingly focused on justice, this demand also served as a powerful political tool, allowing Muawiya to mobilise his considerable resources and rally support against Ali(RA). The demand resonated with many who viewed Uthman(RA)'s assassination as a grave violation of Islamic principles, and others still who sought to exploit the event for political gain.

The Battle of Siffin in 657 CE, a significant turning point in the First Fitna, demonstrates the growing chasm between Ali(RA) and Muawiya regarding political authority and religious interpretation. While the battle itself ended in a stalemate, it significantly altered the political landscape, leading to further polarisation and division within the Muslim community. The arbitration process that followed the battle, intended to resolve the conflict, proved disastrous, fracturing Ali(RA)'s support base and generating further dissent. Many of Ali(RA)'s followers, particularly the Kharijites, rejected the arbitration, viewing it as a compromise of Islamic principles. This ultimately led to the Battle of Nahrawan.

The Kharijites, representing a significant ideological challenge, held a radical interpretation of Islamic law, emphasising strict adherence to religious principles and rejecting perceived compromises. They viewed both Ali(RA) and Muawiya as having deviated from the true path of Islam, viewing arbitration as a form of betrayal. Their strict interpretation of Islamic justice, in contrast to the more pragmatic approaches of other factions, contributed to the violence and unrest characterising the period. They further criticised the existing leadership system, and this rejection of authority and traditional governance would continue to influence subsequent political movements within Islam.

Their rejection of the established leadership, which included Ali(RA), added another layer of complexity to the unfolding conflict.

The Battle of Nahrawan, while seemingly a victory for Ali(RA), intensified the conflict rather than resolving it. The brutal suppression of the Kharijites, while eliminating an immediate military threat, further alienated a substantial segment of the Muslim population. The accusations of excessive violence against surrendered fighters, especially given the Kharijites' fervent religious beliefs and the expectation of mercy within the Islamic faith, played directly into Muawiya's propaganda machine, further discrediting Ali(RA)'s authority and deepening the divisions within the community. The Kharijites, despite their defeat, remained a persistent source of instability and insurgency, reflecting the depth of the religious and ideological fault lines that had split the Muslim world. Despite battlefield losses, their continued existence would demonstrate their influence on later political developments.

The escalating tensions, fueled by religious differences and political machinations, created an atmosphere of profound mistrust and suspicion, making reconciliation increasingly improbable. The Muslim community became deeply fragmented, with loyalties split along regional, tribal, and ideological lines. This fragmentation paralysed the caliphate's capacity to address other pressing challenges, from the administration of the expanding empire to the defence against external enemies. The prolonged conflict consumed resources, time, and energy, weakening the caliphate's overall strength and ability to govern effectively.

The death of Ali(RA), therefore, was not merely a tragic event, but the logical culmination of a series of political and religious divisions that had been festering for years. The assassination, though executed by a single individual, represented the catastrophic failure of the early Islamic state to resolve its internal conflicts peacefully, highlighting the deep fragility of the political order and the vulnerability of the nascent empire to internal strife. It left an enduring legacy of deep divisions, irreconcilable differences, and a power vacuum that would have far-reaching consequences for the future of the Islamic world. The First Fitna was a stark reminder of the inherent challenges in reconciling differing interpretations of religious principles and managing power struggles within a rapidly expanding empire. The consequences of this civil war would reverberate for centuries to come, shaping the political landscape, religious interpretations, and the very fabric of Islamic society.

The Key Players in the First Fitna Ali(RA) Muawiya and their Supporters

The assassination of Uthman(RA) plunged the nascent caliphate into chaos, but the ensuing power vacuum quickly coalesced around two dominant figures: Ali(RA) ibn Abi Talib and Muawiya ibn Abi Sufyan. Their contrasting personalities, political strategies, and support bases defined the First Fitna's trajectory. Ali(RA), the Prophet Muhammad(PBUH)'s cousin and son-in-law, was known for piety and unwavering commitment to Islamic principles. His supporters, predominantly found in Medina and Iraq, saw him as the rightful successor, emphasising his close familial ties to the Prophet and his perceived moral superiority. This claim to legitimacy, however, was not universally accepted and lacked the explicit endorsement of a clear system of succession. His strength lay in his charisma and association with the Prophet, which was often countered by his perceived lack of decisive action in the face of Muawiya's growing power.

His governance style, rooted in his understanding of Islamic justice, lacked the firm administrative hand of his predecessors. He faced constant internal dissent, particularly from the Kharijites, whose radical interpretation of Islamic law clashed with his more pragmatic approach. Moreover, Ali(RA)'s reluctance to confront Muawiya swiftly and decisively, perhaps influenced by his commitment to avoiding further bloodshed within the Muslim community, allowed Muawiya to consolidate his power base in Syria and gain a decisive military advantage. While Ali(RA) commanded considerable loyalty among his followers, the lack of a unified command structure and persistent challenges from within his ranks hampered his ability to counter Muawiya's strategic maneuvers effectively.

Muawiya, the governor of Syria, presented a stark contrast to Ali(RA). A shrewd politician and skilled administrator, he expertly leveraged his position to consolidate his power and challenge Ali(RA)'s claim to the caliphate. His primary strategy focused on exploiting the lingering grievances over Uthman(RA)'s assassination. He skillfully framed his demand for justice against Uthman(RA)'s killers as a quest for upholding Islamic principles and maintaining order. This resonated strongly among many who saw Ali(RA)'s ascension as failing to appropriately address the act, regardless of any personal views on Ali(RA)'s legitimacy as Caliph. This framing allowed Muawiya to mobilise his vast resources and rally support, not just in Syria, but also among various factions who viewed Ali(RA)'s governance with suspicion, either due to his handling of the assassination or concerns about his leadership style.

The First Era of Islamic Leadership

Muawiya's strength resided in his political acumen, efficient administration, and strong military, which he had cultivated in Syria and before the First Fitna, his governance in Syria had been marked by stability and prosperity, creating a strong foundation of loyalty that would prove instrumental in his ability to sustain a prolonged conflict against Ali(RA). He maintained a well-equipped and disciplined army that would become a decisive factor on the battlefield. His ability to harness the resources and manpower of Syria allowed him to wage war on a sustained scale, in contrast to Ali(RA)'s comparatively less stable base in Iraq. His tactical approach involved military strength and effective propaganda, aimed at discrediting Ali(RA) and highlighting his perceived shortcomings. He presented himself as the defender of order and stability, offering a compelling alternative to the perceived chaos under Ali(RA).

The supporters of both Ali(RA) and Muawiya were far from homogeneous entities. Within Ali(RA)'s camp, various groups adhered to differing views and interpretations of Islamic law and governance. The most important Shia unequivocally supported Ali(RA)'s claim to leadership and developed a deep emotional loyalty toward the Alids that would continue to shape their political and religious identity for centuries. This loyalty stemmed from their belief in Ali(RA)'s divinely ordained right to rule and their profound respect for his piety and virtue. The Shia, however, were not a monolithic bloc, and their allegiance to Ali(RA) did not prevent internal disagreements and differing perspectives on strategy and political action.

On the other hand, those who supported Muawiya were a diverse coalition united mainly by their opposition to Ali(RA) and their desire for stability, or at least a different form of leadership after the instability caused by Uthman(RA)'s assassination. This coalition included various tribal groups, administrative officials, and individuals from other regions who felt their interests were better served by Muawiya's governance. Among them, the Umayyad tribe, Muawiya's own, held considerable influence due to its wealth and longstanding political ties. The Umayyads were not inherently favoured across all factions supporting Muawiya, although their numbers and influence would prove critical. The varied backgrounds of Muawiya's supporters also contributed to internal tensions. At the same time, the unifying aspect of their opposition to Ali(RA) bound them together throughout the conflict, allowing Muawiya to maintain a strong, if somewhat fragile, coalition. Such alliances, however, often proved fleeting.

The conflict between Ali(RA) and Muawiya was a struggle for political power and a clash of different approaches to governance, religious interpretations, and social structures. Ali(RA)'s supporters emphasised piety, adherence to Islamic principles, and a sense of community he fostered. Muawiya, on the other hand, championed order, stability, and pragmatism, which resonated amongst those who viewed Ali(RA)'s leadership style as ineffective or inadequate. This clash of perspectives and priorities fueled the escalating conflict, making reconciliation difficult.

The Battle of Siffin in 657 CE is a critical turning point in the First Fitna. The protracted battle, while strategically inconclusive, served as a watershed moment, dividing the Muslim community further and exposing the growing chasm between the competing factions. The subsequent arbitration attempt, intended to resolve the dispute, only exacerbated tensions. Many of Ali(RA)'s followers rejected the outcome, viewing it as a betrayal of Islamic principles and a compromise of justice. This rejection, notably by the Kharijites, led to a further fracturing within Ali(RA)'s already-strained coalition. The emergence of the Kharijites as a distinct political and religious movement represents the most immediate impact of this arbitration failure, leading to the violent Battle of Nahrawan.

The Kharijites' rigorous interpretation of Islamic law and rejection of the established authority further complicated the conflict. Their strict adherence to principles and rejection of political compromise proved a powerful force, further eroding Ali(RA)'s already weakened position and playing into the propaganda efforts of Muawiya. Their extreme views, although representing a minority perspective within the Muslim world, served as a powerful symbol of the religious and political fragmentation that characterised the First Fitna. Their rejection of Ali(RA) and Muawiya highlighted the depth of the political and religious divisions that had shattered the unity of the caliphate.

The assassination of Ali(RA) in 661 CE marked a tragic end to this tumultuous period. While he held a strong base of loyal supporters, he ultimately failed to reconcile the growing fractures within the Muslim community. This failure, while not solely Ali(RA)'s responsibility, resulted from multiple interacting factors: the absence of a clear framework for succession to the caliphate, the lingering resentment over Uthman(RA)'s death, the emergence of differing political and religious interpretations, and the inherent difficulties in governing a vast and diverse empire. Muawiya's eventual victory solidified the Umayyad dynasty's power, shaping the future trajectory of the early Islamic state. However, his victory, achieved amid the devastation of civil war, was a pyrrhic one, leaving behind a legacy of profound division and resentment, setting the stage for future conflicts and challenges to the political order. The First Fitna irrevocably altered the course of early Islamic history, lastingly impacting the Muslim world's political, religious, and social fabric.

Military Campaigns and Battles of the First Fitna

The First Fitna witnessed a series of significant military campaigns and battles that shaped the course of the conflict and profoundly impacted the political landscape of the nascent Islamic empire. These engagements were not merely clashes of arms; they reflected the deep-seated political, religious, and tribal divisions that had fractured the unity of the Caliphate. Understanding these battles is crucial to comprehending the eventual triumph of Muawiya and the establishment of the Umayyad dynasty.

The initial phase of the conflict was characterised by a relatively low-intensity struggle, marked more by political maneuvering and the consolidation of power bases than large-scale warfare. Ali(RA) and Muawiya spent considerable time securing their territories and consolidating their alliances. Ali(RA), based primarily in Iraq, focused on strengthening his regional control. At the same time, Muawiya, from his Syrian stronghold, worked to secure the loyalty of the Syrian army and consolidate resources. This period saw more minor skirmishes and localised conflicts, as both sides tested their strength and gauged the loyalty of their supporters. These early engagements were vital in establishing a military footing and determining the availability of resources for the larger battles. The success of either leader in these early skirmishes would prove crucial in securing the manpower and resources needed to sustain the conflict in the longer term.

The Battle of Siffin, fought in 657 CE near the Euphrates River, is the most pivotal military engagement of the First Fitna. It was a protracted and devastating conflict, lasting for several days and involving tens of thousands of soldiers on both sides. The armies clashed in a series of brutal encounters, displaying the advanced military tactics and weaponry available to the armies of the time. Ali(RA) and Muawiya deployed their forces skillfully, seeking to exploit vulnerabilities and capitalise on tactical advantages. The battle was fierce and bloody, exhibiting the ferocity of the conflict and the depth of the divisions within the Muslim community. The sheer scale of the engagement demonstrates the commitment of both sides and the significance of the conflict for the future of the Caliphate.

The battlefield tactics employed at Siffin revealed the opposing forces' strengths and weaknesses. Ali(RA)'s army, primarily composed of troops loyal to him, fought with fervour but lacked the strong centralised command structure that Muawiya's forces possessed. This difference allowed Muawiya to orchestrate more effective tactical maneuvers and adjust his strategy according to the battlefield situation. Ali(RA)'s reliance on his followers' loyalty and religious zeal often proved a double-edged sword. While this loyalty ensured fierce fighting, it made his troops less adaptable to changing circumstances. The battle's prolonged nature resulted from this contrast in leadership styles and approaches to military strategy.

A key moment in the battle involved raising the Qur'ans on lances by Muawiya's troops. This act, while seemingly pious, served as a clever political maneuver. By invoking the authority of the Quran, Muawiya successfully sowed discord within Ali(RA)'s ranks. Many soldiers in Ali(RA)'s army, questioning the continuation of such a bloody conflict, were persuaded to accept arbitration to resolve the dispute, significantly weakening Ali(RA)'s position. The decision to accept arbitration represented a tactical blunder on Ali(RA)'s part. While intended to spare further bloodshed, it ultimately proved to be disastrous. His opponents saw it as a sign of weakness and fueled Muawiya's narrative of Ali(RA)'s leadership inadequacies.

The aftermath of the Battle of Siffin was as significant as the battle itself. The inconclusive result, rather than ending the conflict, exacerbated the existing tensions and created new fault lines within the Muslim community. Despite its intent to promote peace, the decision to submit to arbitration backfired spectacularly, prompting a significant portion of Ali(RA)'s followers to abandon him. This group, known as the Kharijites, rejected the arbitration process, viewing it as a betrayal of Islamic principles and an illegitimate resolution to the conflict. This development further fragmented the already divided Muslim community, leading to the emergence of a new, radical faction. Their disillusionment with the leadership of both Ali(RA) and Muawiya led to their fierce opposition to both, adding yet another layer of complexity to the already volatile situation.

The Battle of Nahrawan, fought in 658 CE, illuminates the consequences of the failed arbitration at Siffin. This battle pitted Ali(RA)'s forces against the Kharijites, a group fiercely opposed to arbitration and Ali(RA) and Muawiya. The Kharijites, although a smaller force, fought with extraordinary determination, demonstrating their commitment to their radical ideology. Ali(RA), though victorious in this battle, suffered heavy casualties and weakened his already divided army. The brutality of this engagement highlighted the intractable nature of the conflict and the depth of the divisions that fractured the Muslim community. The victory was pyrrhic, damaging Ali(RA)'s image and his standing within the community. It showcased the inability of either side to maintain unity within their camps, reflecting the wider fragmentation engulfing the Caliphate.

The consequences of Nahrawan were profound. While Ali(RA) had suppressed the immediate threat of the Kharijites, the battle further eroded his political standing and weakened his claim to legitimacy. The ruthless suppression of his former followers confirmed the narratives pushed by Muawiya of Ali(RA)'s growing inflexibility and ruthlessness. This narrative further eroded the support of wavering tribes and factions, furthering the decline of his authority. The continuing internal dissent prevented Ali(RA) from focusing on Muawiya, and the continued conflicts weakened his ability to wage an effective campaign against his primary rival.

Beyond these major battles, numerous minor skirmishes and campaigns occurred throughout the First Fitna. These engagements, while often less dramatic than the major battles, played a significant role in shaping the overall trajectory of the conflict. These minor battles usually revolved around local power struggles, tribal loyalties, and control over key resources. They were instrumental in shaping the larger strategic environment, influencing resource availability, and affecting the ability of both sides to sustain the conflict. The combined effect of these more minor engagements ultimately contributed to Muawiya's eventual success in achieving a decisive military advantage.

Muawiya, utilising his superior resources and strategic acumen, effectively exploited the internal divisions within Ali(RA)'s forces. His ability to consolidate his power in Syria and maintain a highly disciplined and well-equipped army gave him a significant military advantage over his opponent. Furthermore, his skilful political maneuvering and propaganda helped undermine Ali(RA)'s authority and erode his support base. Muawiya's focus on maintaining stability and order in his territory contrasted sharply with the ongoing internal conflicts and uncertainty within Ali(RA)'s domains. This further weakened Ali(RA)'s appeal and strengthened Muawiya's narrative of himself as the stability provider.

The assassination of Ali(RA) in 661 CE marked the tragic culmination of the First Fitna. While it did not end the ensuing power struggle between his supporters and Muawiya, it weakened the opposition against the ambitious Syrian governor. The murder of Ali(RA) marked a turning point in the conflict, considerably altering the political landscape. His death removed a unifying figure for a considerable portion of the population, leaving his followers vulnerable. This effectively neutralised a significant source of resistance to Muawiya's ambitions, ultimately paving the way for his victory and establishing the Umayyad dynasty. However, the legacy of the First Fitna's military campaigns and battles was far from settled. The divisions and resentments generated by the conflict continued to shape the political and religious landscape of the early Islamic world for generations to come, leaving an indelible mark on the region's history. The ensuing peace, however fragile, was built on the ashes of civil war and would eventually give way to other conflicts. The consequences of this period of strife were immense, shaping Islam's political, social, and religious trajectory for centuries to follow.

The Impact of the First Fitna on the Political and Religious Landscape of the Islamic World

The First Fitna, while seemingly ending with the assassination of Ali(RA) and the ascension of Muawiya, left an indelible scar on the fabric of the early Islamic world. Its impact transcended the immediate military conflicts, profoundly shaping the political and religious landscape for centuries. The unity, so painstakingly built during the Rashidun Caliphate, was shattered, replaced by deep-seated divisions that would continue to fracture the community. The very concept of the Caliphate, once a symbol of unified Islamic rule, was irrevocably altered, its authority challenged, and its legitimacy questioned.

One of the most significant consequences of the First Fitna was the emergence of distinct political factions. The conflict did not merely pit Ali(RA) against Muawiya; it exposed and exacerbated pre-existing tribal and regional loyalties. The division between the supporters of Ali(RA), based mainly in Iraq and Persia, and those of Muawiya, predominantly from Syria, became entrenched. This regional divergence laid the groundwork for future political conflicts and contributed to the long-term fragmentation of the Islamic empire. The power struggles that followed the Fitna were often defined by these regional identities, hindering the establishment of a unified and centralised authority. The legacy of this division continues to resonate in various regional power dynamics within the Islamic world, proving the persistent impact of this early schism.

The Kharijites, a group that emerged from within Ali(RA)'s ranks, represent a particularly striking consequence of the First Fitna. Their rejection of arbitration at Siffin and their subsequent armed struggle against both Ali(RA) and Muawiya marked a radical departure from the mainstream understanding of Islamic leadership. The Kharijites' insistence on strict adherence to religious principles, coupled with their rejection of any form of compromise, laid the foundation for future extremist movements within Islam. While unsuccessful in their immediate goals, their actions established a tradition of radical dissent that would continue to challenge the political and religious establishment for centuries. Their emphasis on egalitarianism and their rejection of any compromise contributed to the ongoing debate on the interpretation of Islamic law and its application to political authority. Despite its fragmentation into various groups over time, the Kharijite movement demonstrated the enduring impact of the First Fitna on the intellectual and ideological landscape of the Muslim world.

The First Era of Islamic Leadership

The religious implications of the First Fitna were equally profound. The conflict exposed deep disagreements over the interpretation of Islamic law and the proper succession to the Caliphate. While the issue of leadership was a central cause of the war, the underlying tensions reflected broader disputes about the role of religious authority in political life and the extent to which religious principles should dictate political decisions. The ensuing debate over the legitimacy of the various claimants to the Caliphate ignited long-standing controversies that continue to impact discussions surrounding Islamic governance. These debates extended to multiple aspects of Islamic jurisprudence, impacting political issues and matters of personal conduct and social behaviour.

The First Fitna significantly impacted the structure and administration of the early Islamic state. The prolonged conflict disrupted trade routes, hindered administrative functions, and weakened the military might of the Caliphate. The period of instability that followed weakened the central authority, allowing for greater regional autonomy and weakening the administrative capacity of the governing institutions. This fragmentation, in turn, created opportunities for regional governors and influential tribal leaders to exert greater influence, further hindering the consolidation of power under a single ruler. The consequences were far-reaching, leading to a decline in efficiency and weakening the infrastructure supporting the vast empire. This period of turmoil had lasting effects on how the state functioned and its capacity to govern a diverse empire effectively.

The establishment of the Umayyad Caliphate, under Muawiya I, following the assassination of Ali(RA), did not bring an end to the ramifications of the First Fitna. While Muawiya successfully consolidated power and established a new dynasty, the underlying divisions within the Muslim community remained. The Umayyads faced significant opposition, and the tensions between different factions continued to simmer, contributing to future uprisings and rebellions. Muawiya's rule, while considered an era of stability by some, was achieved through considerable political maneuvering and suppression of dissent. This demonstrates that the underlying issues highlighted by the Fitna were not resolved, but rather suppressed, leaving a latent potential for further conflicts. The uneasy peace that followed the First Fitna was a fragile truce, not a resolution.

The First Fitna's impact extended beyond political and religious divisions and had profound social and economic repercussions. The long-term effects included widespread economic disruption, societal instability, and the erosion of trust within the Muslim community. The war resulted in significant loss of life and property, disrupting trade routes and agricultural production. The resulting economic hardship impacted the society on multiple levels, exacerbating existing inequalities and undermining the sense of community that had characterised the Rashidun Caliphate. The trauma inflicted on the community was profound, impacting its social cohesion and exacerbating existing tensions. This societal disintegration and disruption had long-lasting effects, shaping future social and economic development patterns.

The First Era of Islamic Leadership

The legacy of the First Fitna continues to resonate in contemporary interpretations of Islamic history and political thought. The debates surrounding the nature of leadership, the understanding of Islamic law, and the balance between religious and political authority have their roots in the fundamental disagreements that were exposed and exacerbated during this pivotal period. Scholarly discussions continue to grapple with the various interpretations of events, the motives of different actors, and the long-term consequences for the development of Islamic civilisation. The lessons learned from this era remain relevant in examining modern political and religious conflicts, highlighting the enduring significance of the First Fitna's legacy.

The enduring impact of the First Fitna can be seen in the ongoing debates about Islamic governance and the interpretation of religious texts. The conflict exposed the limitations of relying solely on religious principles to resolve political disagreements and the potential for such disputes to escalate into violent confrontations. The subsequent development of Islamic jurisprudence and political philosophy was profoundly shaped by the attempts to learn from past mistakes, especially the failures of resolving the initial conflict through arbitration. The unresolved issues of the Fitna – leadership legitimacy, interpretation of religious texts, and the relationship between religious and political authority – continue to be debated and reinterpreted by Islamic scholars and thinkers. The echoes of the First Fitna resonate in contemporary discussions regarding religious authority, political legitimacy, and the challenges of achieving unity in diverse societies, highlighting the long-lasting effects of this era of strife. Studying the First Fitna remains a crucial lens to understanding the complex dynamics of early Islamic history and the enduring challenges of constructing just and stable societies. Its legacy is a cautionary tale about the dangers of unchecked political ambition, religious extremism, and the fragility of unity in the face of deep-seated divisions.

The Aftermath of the First Fitna A New Era in Islamic History

The assassination of Ali(RA) ibn Abi Talib in 661 CE did not mark the end of the turmoil ignited by the First Fitna. Instead, it ushered in a new era characterised by profound political realignments and fundamentally reshaping the Islamic world's power structures. The immediate aftermath was a scramble for power, with Muawiya I, the governor of Syria and Ali(RA)'s chief opponent, emerging as the victor. His consolidation of power, however, was far from straightforward. The legacy of the Fitna – the deep divisions within the Muslim community, the fracturing of loyalties, and the unresolved questions of legitimacy – continued to cast a long shadow over the nascent Umayyad Caliphate.

Muawiya's rise to power was not simply a matter of military victory. He skillfully employed political strategies, shrewdly forging alliances and neutralising potential rivals. He understood the significance of consolidating his control over key regions and administrative structures. His appointment of loyal governors, often from his tribe, the Quraysh of Mecca, helped to solidify his authority and diminish the influence of competing factions. He also implemented administrative reforms designed to strengthen the central government and reduce the autonomy enjoyed by regional potentates. These measures, however, were often accompanied by the suppression of dissent and the elimination of potential threats to his rule. This centralised approach significantly departed from the relatively decentralised governance that had characterised the Rashidun Caliphate.

The establishment of the Umayyad dynasty brought relative stability, but this stability was fragile and achieved at a cost. The deep-seated divisions that had fueled the First Fitna were not resolved; they were, to a large extent, suppressed. The Umayyad Caliphate faced continuous challenges from internal opposition. The Kharijites, despite their military setbacks, continued their armed struggle, maintaining a persistent threat to the new regime. Their uncompromising ideology, which rejected compromise and emphasised strict adherence to their interpretation of Islamic law, provided a mighty rallying cry for those who felt disenfranchised or marginalised by the Umayyad rule. The Kharijite uprisings, while often localised and ultimately unsuccessful, demonstrated the continuing volatility of the political landscape and the lingering impact of the First Fitna.

The Shi'a community, which had supported Ali(RA) during the Fitna, remained a source of potential opposition. While they didn't engage in widespread rebellion against the Umayyads in the immediate aftermath, their loyalty remained deeply divided, and their resentment of the Umayyads persisted. The Shi'a's belief in the legitimacy of Ali(RA) and his descendants as rightful successors to the Caliphate posed a long-term challenge to the Umayyad claim to power, setting the stage for future conflicts and shaping the religious and political identity of the Shi'a community for centuries to come. This ongoing tension illustrates how the First Fitna created lasting religious and political divides far beyond the immediate conflict.

The consequences of the First Fitna extended beyond the political sphere. The prolonged conflict had devastating economic repercussions. Trade routes were disrupted, agricultural production suffered, and the overall economic vitality of the empire declined. This financial hardship exacerbated existing social inequalities, creating insecurity and instability within the broader community. The loss of life and the destruction of infrastructure further compounded the economic crisis, leaving lasting scars on the economic fabric of the newly established Caliphate. The financial difficulties of the empire impacted everything from public works projects to the military's ability to maintain its strength, contributing to vulnerabilities that would be exploited later.

Furthermore, the First Fitna profoundly impacted the social fabric of early Islamic society. The deep divisions within the community undermined the sense of unity and collective purpose that had characterised the Rashidun Caliphate. The prolonged conflict and the resulting violence eroded trust, leading to social fragmentation and an increase in inter-tribal tensions. The trauma experienced during the Fitna had lasting psychological and social implications, affecting relationships between individuals and communities for generations to come. The wounds inflicted by the Fitna ran deep and profoundly impacted societal cohesion.

The administrative and military consequences of the First Fitna were equally significant. The prolonged conflict severely weakened the central government's capacity to govern the vast empire effectively. The administrative infrastructure, already strained by the rapid expansion of the Caliphate, suffered further damage due to the protracted conflict. The disruption of administrative channels hindered the collection of taxes and the enforcement of laws, contributing to a decline in central authority and increased regional autonomy. The military, too, was significantly weakened, having suffered heavy casualties and losing considerable manpower. This military vulnerability would have consequences for future conflicts and ultimately influence the trajectory of the empire.

Though successful in consolidating power, the Umayyad Caliphate inherited a fractured and unstable state. Muawiya I and his successors faced the constant challenge of controlling a diverse empire marked by deep-seated regional and religious divisions. This is reflected in the policies adopted by the Umayyads, which often involved a delicate balance between consolidating central authority and managing internal opposition. The Umayyads employed strategies to maintain their power, including strategic appointments, extensive intelligence networks, and brutal suppression of rebellions. The need to continually address the unresolved issues stemming from the First Fitna shaped the Umayyad agenda and played a significant role in the evolution of the Caliphate.

The legacy of the First Fitna extends far beyond the events of the mid-7th century. The religious and political divisions that arose during this period continued to shape the development of Islamic civilisation for centuries. The emergence of distinct theological schools and legal interpretations reflected the enduring influence of the debates and disagreements sparked by the conflict. The very concept of the Caliphate was irrevocably altered, its authority challenged, and its legitimacy questioned. The deep-seated mistrust and rivalry between different factions continued to fuel political conflict, shaping the dynamics of power within the Muslim world for generations to come. This conflict left a profound mark on how Islamic political theory and practice developed, shaping future debates on authority, governance and religious interpretation.

The First Fitna serves as a crucial case study in the complexities of early Islamic history, and its ramifications continue to resonate in contemporary interpretations of Islamic history and political thought. It highlights the inherent dangers of unchecked political ambition, religious extremism, and the fragility of unity in the face of deep-seated divisions. Scholars continue to debate the long-term consequences of the First Fitna, exploring the various interpretations of events and the impact on the development of Islamic jurisprudence, political theory, and social structures. Studying this pivotal period offers valuable insights into the dynamics of early Islamic governance and the enduring challenges of constructing just and stable societies. Understanding the First Fitna and its aftermath is essential for a comprehensive understanding of the evolution of the Islamic world, its diverse religious and political traditions, and the long-lasting impact of internal conflict on the trajectory of an empire. Its lessons remain relevant today, reminding us of the dangers of unchecked power, the importance of inclusive governance, and the enduring challenges of reconciling religious piety with political realities.

Chapter 5
The Legacy of the Rashidun Caliphate: A Foundation for Islamic Governance and its Lasting Influence

The Administrative and Legal Innovations of the Rashidun Caliphate

The Rashidun Caliphate, despite its relatively short lifespan of just twenty-nine years, witnessed a period of remarkable administrative and legal innovation that laid the groundwork for centuries of Islamic governance. The four Rightly Guided Caliphs—Abu Bakr(RA), Umar(RA), Uthman(RA), and Ali(RA)—each contributed to the development of a system that, while evolving, possessed crucial characteristics that distinguished it from earlier models of governance and profoundly influenced subsequent Islamic states. This innovative system wasn't built in a vacuum; it emerged from the practical necessities of managing a rapidly expanding empire, resolving internal conflicts, and administering a diverse population adhering to a newly established faith.

Establishing a centralised administration was a key achievement of the Rashidun era. Before the advent of Islam, the Arabian Peninsula was characterised by a

The Administrative and Legal Innovations of the Rashidun Caliphate

fragmented political landscape of tribes and independent city-states. The rapid expansion of the Islamic empire after the Prophet Muhammad(PBUH)'s death presented an unprecedented administrative challenge. Abu Bakr(RA), the first caliph, faced the immediate crisis of the Ridda Wars, rebellions by tribes who rejected the new faith. His swift and decisive military response secured the nascent Islamic state and demonstrated the importance of a centralised command structure capable of effective mobilisation and resource allocation. The efficient organisation of the army, with its standardised tactics and logistics, laid the foundation for the future military successes of the Rashidun Caliphate and highlighted the critical link between military strength and administrative capability.

Umar(RA) ibn al-Khattab, the second caliph, is widely credited with developing a more sophisticated and comprehensive administrative system. His reign saw the establishment of a formal bureaucracy, staffed by competent officials responsible for collecting taxes, managing public works, and maintaining order. He divided the vast empire into provinces governed by a designated official who reported directly to the caliph. This system ensured greater accountability and streamlined the administration of a vastly expanding territory. Umar(RA)'s innovations extended to establishing a postal service for efficient communication across the empire, a crucial element in maintaining control and facilitating the flow of information to and from the central authority. The establishment of a sophisticated system of accounting and record-keeping contributed to financial stability and

The Administrative and Legal Innovations of the Rashidun Caliphate

enabled efficient resource management. For its time, this administrative system was remarkably effective in managing diverse populations and ensuring the smooth functioning of the burgeoning state.

Implementing a just and equitable tax system was another significant administrative achievement of the Rashidun Caliphate. Umar(RA)'s tax reforms, particularly the implementation of the *jizya* (poll tax levied on non-Muslims) and the *kharaj* (land tax), constituted a crucial element in the financial stability of the empire. While the system certainly generated revenue, the emphasis on fairness and the careful consideration of local circumstances marked a sharp departure from the often arbitrary and exploitative practices of previous rulers. The system allowed for exemptions based on need and age, ensuring that the burdens of taxation were distributed equitably, as far as was possible, across the diverse population. The meticulous record-keeping associated with tax collection ensured transparency and reduced opportunities for corruption. The efficient collection of taxes was pivotal in funding the empire's military campaigns, public works projects, and social welfare programs. The structure ensured that revenue was collected and fairly distributed among the populace, enhancing the stability and overall governance of the Rashidun era.

The legal innovations of the Rashidun Caliphate were equally groundbreaking. While the Quran served as the ultimate source of law, its interpretations and applications required careful consideration and adaptation to diverse situations. The process of *ijma* (consensus of the learned)

The Administrative and Legal Innovations of the Rashidun Caliphate

and *qiyas* (analogical reasoning) played a crucial role in developing Islamic jurisprudence during this period. This emphasis on legal interpretation and adaptation was vital in establishing a legal framework appropriate to a large and complex empire. The legal innovations of the Rashidun Caliphate did not merely involve interpreting religious texts, but also dealt with the practical matters of civil law, commercial disputes, criminal justice, and property rights. These aspects were vital in establishing a predictable and orderly system of law that contributed significantly to social stability and economic prosperity. The early emphasis on establishing a functioning legal framework based on interpretation and consensus laid the foundation for the later development of Islamic legal schools (madhhabs), which were critical in shaping Islamic jurisprudence for centuries.

The caliphs' focus on justice and fairness was another defining characteristic of their governance. They established systems to address grievances, providing mechanisms for citizens to appeal decisions and ensure the fair treatment of all within the empire. This commitment to justice was vital in building trust between the ruling elite and the population. While the empire undeniably expanded through military conquest, the caliphs attempted to promote a degree of social and religious harmony. The relative religious tolerance granted to non-Muslims, particularly the 'People of the Book' (Jews and Christians), while not always consistently applied, represented a noteworthy departure from many other empires of the time. This policy, intended to foster a degree of peaceful

The Administrative and Legal Innovations of the Rashidun Caliphate

coexistence, helped establish a sense of relative stability within the diverse populations of the empire. This relative stability facilitated commerce and fostered a certain degree of cultural exchange, further contributing to the overall prosperity and integration of the diverse peoples under their rule.

The Rashidun Caliphate's administrative and legal innovations were not without their challenges. The rapid expansion of the empire placed immense strain on administrative resources. The difficulties in controlling and managing such vast and distant territories were frequently tested, leading to occasional abuses of power and instances of injustice. The rise of internal conflicts during the later years of the Rashidun Caliphate exposed vulnerabilities in the system, especially regarding succession issues and competing interpretations of Islamic law. These challenges ultimately contributed to the First Fitna, the devastating civil war that ended the Rashidun period. However, despite these internal struggles, the administrative structures and legal principles established during this era proved remarkably durable.

Despite the turmoil that followed, the basic administrative framework and the emphasis on just governance established during the Rashidun era had a lasting impact on the development of subsequent Islamic states. Many of the administrative practices and legal principles developed during this time, such as the organisation of provinces, the systems of taxation, and the emphasis on legal interpretation and consensus, served as models for later Islamic empires, regardless of their specific political structures. The concept of a centralised, yet relatively just and equitable, state played an essential role in Islamic political thought.

The legacy of the Rashidun Caliphate extends beyond its administrative and legal systems. It represents an early attempt to synthesise religious principles with practical governance. The caliphs faced the immense challenge of building a cohesive and just society from a diverse range of social groups, religious beliefs, and cultural practices, all within the context of a rapid expansion. Their achievements and failures provide a valuable lens through which to understand the early development of Islamic civilisation and the ongoing challenges of governance in diverse and rapidly changing societies. Despite being imperfect, the principles and structures they established contributed substantially to shaping the course of Islamic governance for centuries, serving as a benchmark for later Islamic states and a constant point of reference in discussions on justice, governance, and Islamic law. The Rashidun era, though relatively brief, serves as a crucial foundation for understanding the complexities and continuities in the rich history of Islamic political thought and practice. Its impact reverberates throughout history, influencing the Islamic world's political and legal landscape and continuing to inform contemporary debates on governance and justice.

The Expansion and Consolidation of Islamic Rule

The astonishingly swift expansion of the Rashidun Caliphate, a phenomenon unparalleled in speed and scale during that era, profoundly shaped the political and cultural landscape of the Near East and beyond. This expansion, fueled by religious fervour, skilled military leadership, and internal weaknesses within the existing Byzantine and Sasanian empires, fundamentally altered the geopolitical map and had lasting implications for the development of Islamic civilisation. The conquests were not simply acts of military prowess; they were deeply intertwined with the political and administrative strategies of the caliphs, defining the very nature of the emerging Islamic state.

The military success of the Rashidun armies stemmed from several key factors. Firstly, the newly unified Arab tribes, energised by their shared faith and the promise of reward in this life and the hereafter, possessed unparalleled motivation. Unlike the professional, but often demoralised, armies of the Byzantine and Sasanian empires, the Rashidun forces were composed of soldiers who fought with intense religious conviction, believing they were engaged in a divinely ordained mission. This fervour translated into remarkable battlefield discipline and resilience, enabling them to overcome numerically superior foes.

Secondly, the Rashidun armies benefited from shrewd military leadership. Figures like Khalid ibn al-Walid, a renowned military strategist, demonstrated exceptional tactical acumen, employing innovative strategies and adapting to diverse battlefield conditions. Their mastery of desert warfare and the effective utilisation of cavalry proved decisive in many crucial battles. The careful planning and execution of campaigns, combined with efficient logistics and supply lines, were essential for their success, particularly in the face of protracted campaigns far from their base of operations.

The conquest of Syria, which began under Abu Bakr(RA) and continued under Umar(RA), showcased the effectiveness of Rashidun military strategies. The battles of Yarmouk (636 CE) and Ajnadayn (634 CE) were pivotal victories that significantly weakened the Byzantine Empire. These victories opened access to rich and fertile lands, providing the expanding Caliphate with substantial resources and laying the foundation for further expansion. The conquest of Syria was not merely a military campaign but also a strategic maneuver aimed at securing access to trade routes and controlling vital territories. The subsequent integration of Syria into the Caliphate presented considerable administrative challenges, but its incorporation provided access to wealth and manpower. The skilled use of existing infrastructure and the incorporation of local expertise were instrumental in ensuring a reasonably smooth transition and the long-term stability of the conquered region.

The conquest of Persia under Umar(RA) followed a similar pattern, although it faced different challenges. The Sasanian Empire, despite its internal weaknesses, presented a formidable foe. Yet, the Rashidun armies, despite facing tough resistance, achieved decisive victories at the battles of al-Qādisiyyah (636 CE) and Nahavand (642 CE). These battles crushed the Sasanian military and dealt a fatal blow to the empire's prestige and authority. This conquest also gave access to Mesopotamia and Persia's extensive resources and a substantial population, considerably increasing the growing empire's demographic strength. The administrative integration of Persia proved more complex than Syria's due to the more intricate societal and political structures. Still, the Rashidun caliphs implemented successful strategies that mitigated significant conflict and helped ensure the region's long-term stability.

The rapid territorial expansion of the Rashidun Caliphate posed significant administrative challenges. The conquered territories were immensely diverse, encompassing different cultures, languages, and religious beliefs. The caliphs, however, developed ingenious administrative systems to manage this diversity. They established a network of governors to oversee the provinces, maintaining a delicate

The Expansion and Consolidation of Islamic Rule

balance between centralisation and decentralisation. While often leading to tensions and challenges, this approach allowed for a degree of autonomy within regions while ensuring overall loyalty to the central caliphate.

Integrating non-Arab populations was a key feature of the Rashidun Caliphate's administrative policies. The 'People of the Book' (Jews and Christians) were generally granted a degree of religious tolerance, though subject to the payment of the *jizya* tax. While reflecting a pragmatic approach to ruling a diverse population, this policy also had limitations. Applying the *jizya* tax was not always consistent, and discrimination occurred. This reflects the complexities of implementing consistent policies across a vast, diverse, and rapidly acquired territory.

The economic consequences of the expansion were substantial. The conquered territories provided the Rashidun Caliphate with access to immense wealth. This wealth facilitated further military expansion and fueled the development of infrastructure and social programs within the Caliphate. This growth, however, did not benefit all equally. While specific segments of the population thrived, issues of social and economic inequality began to emerge, contributing to growing societal divisions that would later play a role in exacerbating internal conflicts.

The religious and cultural implications of the expansion were profound. The spread of Islam was deeply intertwined with the military conquests. While conversion to Islam was not universally enforced, many people embraced the new faith, either through coercion, persuasion, or a genuine

The Expansion and Consolidation of Islamic Rule

belief in its message. This process significantly reshaped the region's religious landscape, creating a new synthesis of existing traditions and Islamic practices. This resulted in significant cultural exchange, as diverse populations interacted, impacting various aspects of life, from art and architecture to literature and scholarship.

Therefore, the expansion of the Rashidun Caliphate was a complex and multifaceted phenomenon. It was not simply a military campaign, but a process of territorial acquisition, administrative innovation, cultural exchange, and religious transformation. The speed and scale of the expansion were remarkable achievements, yet they also created immense challenges and laid the seeds for future conflicts. The challenges of integrating such vast and diverse territories, managing a rapidly expanding bureaucracy, and maintaining social harmony within an increasingly complex empire ultimately contributed to the internal tensions that would eventually shatter the Rashidun Caliphate. Nonetheless, the legacy of this period of expansion remains profound, reshaping the region's political, cultural, and religious landscape for centuries to come. However imperfectly implemented, the administrative frameworks, the military innovations, and the integration policies left an indelible mark on the subsequent development of the Islamic world and continue to be studied and debated today.

The Development of Islamic Law and Jurisprudence during the Rashidun Era

The rapid expansion of the Rashidun Caliphate brought an unprecedented need for a robust and adaptable legal framework. The diverse populations under their rule—Arabs, Persians, Byzantines, and various other groups—practised different legal systems and customs. The challenge for the Rashidun caliphs was not merely to conquer but also to govern effectively, and this required the creation of a system of law capable of adjudicating disputes and maintaining order across a vast and heterogeneous empire. The era saw the initial stages in the development of Islamic jurisprudence, drawing upon pre-Islamic Arab traditions, scriptural interpretations of the Quran and the Sunnah (the Prophet Muhammad(PBUH)'s teachings and practices), and the wisdom of learned companions of the Prophet.

Abu Bakr(RA), the first caliph, faced immediate challenges upon assuming leadership. The death of the Prophet had created a power vacuum, and several tribes revolted against the nascent Caliphate in what became known as the Ridda Wars (Wars of Apostasy). Though fraught with conflict, this period shaped early Islamic law. Abu Bakr(RA)'s decisions regarding the treatment of these rebellious tribes based on his interpretations of Islamic principles and the prevailing circumstances set precedents that profoundly influenced subsequent legal interpretations. His approach, prioritising the unity of the nascent Islamic community and the enforcement of the newly established political system, was essential in solidifying the Caliphate's foundations and establishing necessary legal groundwork. While he didn't codify a formal legal system, his rulings during this chaotic period became crucial building blocks for future Islamic jurisprudence. His reliance on consensus (ijma) among the senior companions of the Prophet was a key element of his decision-making and laid the groundwork for the importance of communal agreement in Islamic legal reasoning.

The reign of Umar(RA) ibn al-Khattab, the second caliph, witnessed a period of consolidation and significant administrative reform. Recognising the need for a more systematic approach to governance, Umar(RA) oversaw the development of a more formalised administrative structure. This necessitated the expansion and systematisation of legal procedures and the establishment of courts to resolve disputes. While not a codified legal system in the modern sense, Umar(RA)'s rulings established precedents for handling various issues, from taxation and land ownership to criminal justice and commercial transactions. His emphasis on justice, fairness, and meticulous attention to detail significantly influenced Islamic legal principles. A key aspect of Umar(RA)'s contribution was developing the *qadis* system, establishing a network of judges across the Caliphate responsible for applying the law and settling disputes. Drawing from their understanding of the Quran, Sunnah, and customary law, these qadis were vital in ensuring justice and maintaining order throughout the vast and expanding territory. His emphasis on practicality and his focus on resolving disputes fairly and efficiently contributed to the acceptance and effectiveness of the fledgling legal system.

Uthman(RA) ibn Affan, the third caliph, continued the work of his predecessors, focusing on consolidating and refining the legal and administrative frameworks. He emphasised consolidating existing practices and ensuring consistency in their application across the Caliphate. While Uthman(RA)'s reign also saw increased internal conflicts, his contributions to the development of Islamic law were primarily indirect, focusing on strengthening the administrative framework within which legal decisions were made and carried out. This implied a focus on standardising procedures and enhancing the capacity of the administrative bodies responsible for the implementation of legal decisions, an essential contribution to solidifying the nascent legal system's effectiveness. His efforts to standardise the Quran were crucial in supporting the integrity of the primary source for Islamic law, ensuring uniformity and removing potential discrepancies in the text. This indirectly strengthened the foundation upon which later legal interpretations would be built.

Ali(RA) ibn Abi Talib, the fourth caliph, faced significant challenges upon assuming leadership, facing opposition and ultimately succumbing to assassination. His reign is marked by the escalating First Fitna, a devastating civil war that significantly destabilised the Caliphate. While his contributions to legal development during this turbulent period were limited, his emphasis on the importance of just governance and his commitment to scholarly debate on legal matters were significant. His perspectives on legal interpretation helped shape later debates within Islamic legal schools of thought, demonstrating that legal and scholarly debates continued to influence legal development even during intense political conflict. The issues debated during this period, dealing with the legitimacy of governance and the interpretation of religious texts, had long-lasting implications for the future of Islamic law and politics. The disputes of his reign highlighted the importance of careful. They considered the interpretation of sacred texts and the continuous need for scholars and leaders to engage in reasoned debate to arrive at just solutions.

During the Rashidun era, the primary sources of Islamic law were the Quran and the Sunnah. The Quran, considered the ultimate divine revelation, was the supreme authority. The Sunnah, encompassing the Prophet Muhammad(PBUH)'s sayings, actions, and tacit approvals, provided essential guidance for interpreting and applying the Quran's principles to practical situations. However, the interpretation and application of these sources were not always straightforward. Ambiguities and contradictions often emerged, necessitating careful consideration of context and various interpretative methodologies.

One key method of interpretation was *ijma*, or consensus among the community's scholars and leaders. This process played a crucial role in resolving disagreements and establishing legal precedents. Another significant method was *qiyas*, analogical reasoning, where legal rulings for new cases were derived by drawing parallels to existing ones. This method allowed for flexibility and adaptability in handling novel situations, demonstrating the dynamism of early Islamic jurisprudence. The importance of scholarly interpretation and legal reasoning is evident in the Rashidun Caliphate. The emphasis on establishing precedents and the methods developed for resolving ambiguous interpretations laid the foundation for the later legal schools of thought (madhhabs) that emerged.

The development of Islamic law during the Rashidun Caliphate was not a monolithic process. It involved continuous debate, negotiation, and the application of various interpretive methods. The decisions made by the caliphs, though not always formally codified, laid the foundation for subsequent legal developments and demonstrated the fundamental principles of Islamic jurisprudence. The emphasis on justice, fairness, and the consistent application of the Quran and Sunnah became cornerstones of the evolving legal system. While facing challenges and changing throughout this period, the administrative structures put into place provided the necessary framework for applying and interpreting the law, establishing courts and judicial processes that would leave a lasting mark on the Islamic world. While imperfect and subject to the realities of a rapidly expanding and diverse empire, these nascent legal structures successfully managed the administration of justice and the governance of diverse populations, thereby setting the stage for further development of Islamic jurisprudence in subsequent centuries. The legacy of the Rashidun era is not merely one of military conquest but also the essential groundwork laid for developing a dynamic and enduring legal system. The challenges and innovations of this period continue to inform scholarly debates and legal practices in the Islamic world today.

The Social and Cultural Impacts of the Rashidun Caliphate

The rapid expansion of the Rashidun Caliphate, fueled by military successes, had profound and multifaceted social and cultural consequences. The impact extended far beyond the purely political, reshaping the social fabric of the Arab world and the newly conquered territories. The initial phase was marked by the swift spread of Islam, not solely through conquest but also the persuasive power of its message and the relative tolerance shown to non-Muslim subjects (dhimmis) under the early Caliphate. This period, however, was not without its complexities, as the integration of diverse cultures and the establishment of a new social order posed significant challenges.

The conversion to Islam was a gradual process, influenced by various factors. For some, particularly amongst the previously marginalised groups within Arab society, the egalitarian message of Islam offered a powerful alternative to existing social hierarchies. The promise of community, justice, and spiritual fulfilment proved highly attractive, fostering a sense of belonging that transcended tribal affiliations. In contrast, the conversion process in newly conquered territories was often more complex and varied. While some embraced Islam voluntarily, lured by its appeal or motivated by pragmatic considerations, others converted under duress or as a means of avoiding heavier taxation or social persecution. The level of coercion varied across different regions and periods, and scholarly debate persists on the exact nature and extent of such pressures. Nevertheless, the rate at which Islam spread across the vast territories within and beyond the Arabian Peninsula is a significant achievement during this period and a testament to the effectiveness of the early Islamic missionary efforts.

The interaction between Arab culture and those of the conquered territories led to a dynamic exchange of ideas and practices. Persia and Byzantium's relatively advanced administrative systems and intellectual traditions considerably influenced the nascent Islamic state. Persian administrative models, particularly in areas like tax collection and bureaucratic organisation, were adopted and adapted to fit the needs of the growing Caliphate. This adoption, often involving a fusion of Islamic principles with pre-existing practices, reflects the pragmatism and adaptability of the Rashidun rulers. Likewise, the intellectual legacy of the conquered regions contributed significantly to the development of Islamic scholarship. Many non-Arab scholars, particularly those from Persia and Syria, actively participated in the translation and

The Social and Cultural Impacts of the Rashidun Caliphate

dissemination of classical knowledge, enriching the cultural landscape of the Caliphate. This collaborative learning experience laid the groundwork for the golden age of Islamic science and philosophy, which would flourish in the following centuries.

The cultural integration, however, was not without its challenges. The rapid expansion of Arab power led to tensions between the ruling Arab elite and the subject populations. While the Rashidun caliphs generally adopted a relatively tolerant policy towards non-Muslims, maintaining the *dhimmi* system with its associated taxes and legal limitations, instances of conflict and discrimination were unavoidable. The differences in social customs, legal practices, and religious beliefs often created friction, and the administration of justice under the new system was a constant source of negotiation and adaptation. The tension between the Arab conquerors and the conquered populations would persist for generations and play a significant role in subsequent periods' political and social upheavals.

The development of early Islamic society under the Rashidun Caliphate was characterised by a remarkable degree of social mobility. The pre-Islamic tribal structure, with its rigid social hierarchy, was gradually replaced by a more meritocratic system based on religious piety and service to the state. This does not imply the complete erasure of tribal identities, however. Tribal affiliations played a significant role in social organisation, especially kinship and loyalty. However, the emphasis on Islamic principles of equality and justice created opportunities for

The Social and Cultural Impacts of the Rashidun Caliphate

advancement for those who demonstrated faith and skill, irrespective of their tribal origins. Though gradual and uneven, this shift reflected the social transformation engendered by the spread of Islam, with religious identity gradually becoming more prominent than pre-existing tribal identities.

The economic consequences of the Rashidun expansion were substantial. The newly conquered territories brought immense wealth into the Caliphate, fueling economic growth and the expansion of trade networks. Unifying diverse regions under a single administration facilitated trade, reducing internal tariffs and fostering economic exchange between East and West. This resulted in the growth of cities and the emergence of significant commercial centres, benefiting both Arab and non-Arab merchants. The standardisation of coinage and the implementation of equitable taxation systems created economic stability, contributing to the overall prosperity of the Caliphate. However, this economic prosperity was not evenly distributed, with some regions and groups benefiting more. The management of the vast economic resources of the Caliphate and the fair distribution of wealth remained a constant challenge throughout the Rashidun era, influencing the social and political landscape of the Caliphate significantly.

The standardisation of the Quran under Uthman(RA), a crucial event in early Islamic history, profoundly impacted the expanding Caliphate's cultural unity. Various textual variations across different communities posed a potential threat to religious unity, which was carefully addressed by standardising the text. The standardised Quran became the cornerstone of Islamic religious practice, creating a shared cultural and spiritual identity across the diverse populations within the Caliphate. This cultural unification through a standardised religious text played an essential role in maintaining the stability and cohesion of the empire, shaping the development of Islamic society and culture for centuries.

The Rashidun Caliphate's legacy extends far beyond its military conquests. The period saw the establishment of fundamental institutions of Islamic governance, the formulation of early Islamic jurisprudence, and the initial steps towards creating a unified Islamic culture. The cultural exchanges between diverse communities brought about a dynamic interplay of ideas, practices, and traditions, shaping the cultural identity of the Islamic world. While the era ended with the First Fitna, its impact on the subsequent development of Islamic civilisation was indelible. The administrative and legal structures, the methods of interpreting religious texts, and the socio-political norms that began to take shape during this period laid the foundation for the later intellectual and cultural flourishing of the Islamic golden age. The lasting impact of the Rashidun Caliphate on Islamic governance and its enduring influence on subsequent cultural developments serve as a testament to its importance in shaping the Islamic world. This era's social and cultural transformations continue to shape debates and scholarship on early Islam. Its complexity and achievements provide rich grounds for continued study and understanding.

The Enduring Legacy Lessons from the Rashidun Caliphate for Modern Governance

The Rashidun Caliphate, despite its relatively short lifespan of 29 years, left an indelible mark on the course of Islamic history and continues to offer valuable insights for contemporary governance. Its legacy transcends the purely political, encompassing significant advancements in jurisprudence, administration, and social organisation. Examining the successes and failures of the four Rightly Guided Caliphs – Abu Bakr(RA), Umar(RA), Uthman(RA), and Ali(RA) – reveals critical lessons applicable to modern leadership and pursuing just and equitable societies.

One of the most striking aspects of the Rashidun Caliphate was its emphasis on consultation (shura). While the Caliph held ultimate authority, seeking counsel from advisors and community leaders was integral to decision-making. Abu Bakr(RA), for instance, famously convened a council of prominent Companions to determine the succession after the Prophet Muhammad(PBUH)'s death, a process that, while contentious, established a precedent for collective deliberation in governance. Umar(RA), known for his practical wisdom and administrative acumen, frequently consulted with his advisors, demonstrating a willingness to consider diverse perspectives. This consultative approach fostered a sense of shared responsibility and legitimacy, enhancing the Caliph's authority while mitigating the risks of arbitrary rule. Modern governance systems would greatly benefit from embracing such participatory approaches, fostering inclusivity and broader public buy-in to crucial decisions. While the sheer scale and complexity of modern states necessitate a more intricate framework of consultation, the fundamental principle of seeking diverse viewpoints and incorporating them into policy remains vital.

The Rashidun Caliphs also displayed remarkable administrative efficiency, particularly in managing the rapidly expanding empire. Umar(RA) ibn al-Khattab, often considered the most successful administrator amongst the four, implemented various administrative reforms that significantly strengthened the Caliphate's infrastructure. He established a sophisticated taxation system, ensuring a fair and equitable distribution of resources. Establishing a postal service and standardised weights and measures facilitated trade and communication throughout the vast territory. Furthermore, Umar(RA)'s attention to detail in appointing qualified officials, regardless of tribal affiliation, demonstrated a commitment to meritocracy. He established a robust system of provincial governance, assigning governors responsible for managing their respective provinces with clear guidelines and regular accountability measures. This approach contrasts starkly with many contemporary states plagued by corruption and inefficiency. The emphasis on competence and transparency in governance during the Rashidun era offers a stark reminder of the importance of good governance in ensuring stability, progress, and the welfare of the citizenry.

The development and application of early Islamic jurisprudence is another significant legacy. The Rashidun period witnessed the initial codification of Islamic law, building upon the principles derived from the Quran and the Sunnah (Prophet Muhammad(PBUH)'s teachings and practices). Scholars of Fiqh (Islamic jurisprudence) such as Abdullah ibn Mas'ud and Ibn Abbas played crucial roles in interpreting Islamic law and applying it to the early Islamic community's challenges. The emphasis on consensus (ijma) and analogical reasoning (qiyas) laid the foundations of the evolving legal system. The Rashidun Caliphs played a vital role in overseeing this development, upholding the rule of law and ensuring the consistency of its application across the Caliphate. This period serves as a crucial formative stage in the development of Islamic jurisprudence and demonstrates the intricate interplay between religious principles and their practical application in governance. This emphasis on robust legal frameworks and a just judicial system remains a cornerstone of good governance today.

The Rashidun Caliphs also addressed the challenges of societal integration and diversity. The swift expansion of the Caliphate brought together diverse communities with differing cultural backgrounds, religious beliefs, and legal traditions. While instances of conflict and discrimination existed, the general policy of the early Caliphs towards non-Muslim subjects (dhimmis) was one of relative tolerance. The *dhimmi* system, while characterised by certain legal limitations and higher taxation, offered a degree of protection and allowed non-Muslims to practice their faith relatively freely. The implementation of this system reflects the effort to build a pluralistic society where different religious communities could coexist, albeit within the framework of a dominant Islamic political structure. The success in managing such diversity, despite its inherent shortcomings, offers important lessons for modern societies grappling with issues of multiculturalism and integration.

However, the Rashidun Caliphate's history was not without its challenges. Internal conflicts and succession crises ultimately led to the First Fitna, a devastating civil war severely weakening the Caliphate. The events surrounding the deaths of Uthman(RA) and the ensuing conflict with Ali(RA) highlight the dangers of political instability, factionalism, and the fragility of power transitions. The lessons drawn from this period emphasise the need for robust institutional mechanisms to manage succession, prevent internal conflict, and ensure peaceful power transfer. Furthermore, the failure to adequately address simmering grievances and tribal loyalties and the uneven distribution of power contributed significantly to the descent into chaos. These aspects of the Caliphate's demise serve as cautionary tales for modern political systems, highlighting the critical need for transparent and inclusive governance structures, designed to ensure stability and to mitigate against the potential for conflict. Effective institutions and processes of conflict resolution and power transition are crucial to ensuring the enduring success of any governance system.

The legacy of the Rashidun Caliphate extends far beyond its administrative and legal achievements. Its emphasis on justice, consultation, and the rule of law resonates in contemporary political thought. While rooted in a specific historical and religious context, the Caliphate's governance model offers valuable lessons for modern leaders grappling with social justice, economic development, and political stability issues. The challenges faced during this era, such as managing diversity, ensuring equitable resource distribution, and establishing mechanisms for peaceful succession, remain strikingly relevant today. The ability of the early caliphs to consolidate a vast and diverse empire, create a cohesive administrative system, and establish a framework for Islamic jurisprudence provides invaluable insights into leadership, governance, and the building of inclusive societies. Its successes and failures offer an enduring testament to human governance's challenges, complexities, and potential. Therefore, studying the Rashidun Caliphate is not merely a historical exercise but a crucial undertaking with significant implications for understanding today's enduring pursuit of just and equitable governance. Exploring these challenges and the lessons learned during this era can contribute significantly to informed and effective governance in the modern world.

Acknowledgments

This project would not have been possible without the support, companionship, and thoughtful engagement of many individuals.

I am incredibly grateful to the many friends—Muslim and non-Muslim alike—whose curiosity, questions, reflections, and challenges inspired this work. Our conversations, whether over meals, on walks, or during moments of quiet contemplation, often evolved into dialogues that deepened my understanding and broadened my perspective.

To those with whom I have shared the rhythms of daily life—discussing, debating, worshipping, arguing, laughing, and learning together—you have helped shape the ideas in this book and the spirit in which they were written. Your openness, sincerity, and willingness to explore complex and sometimes uncomfortable questions were a source of genuine motivation throughout this journey.

To my family and close companions: thank you for your unwavering patience, encouragement, and love as I immersed myself in this demanding work.

Any faults or shortcomings that remain are entirely my own.

Glossary

Caliph: The title of the head of state in an Islamic state.

Dhimmi: A non-Muslim living under Islamic rule, granted protection under specific legal terms.

Fiqh: Islamic jurisprudence.

Fitna: Civil strife or discord, often referring to the major internal conflicts in early Islamic history.

Ijma: Consensus amongst Islamic scholars on a point of law.

Qiyas: Analogical reasoning in Islamic jurisprudence.

Ridda Wars: Wars fought by the first Caliph, Abu Bakr(RA), against various Arabian tribes that rebelled after the death of the Prophet Muhammad(PBUH).

Shura: Consultation; a process of seeking counsel from advisors and community leaders.

Glossary

Sunnah: The teachings and practices of the Prophet Muhammad(PBUH).

About Author

Dr. Shaikh Mohammad Shahriyar Wahab was born in Bangladesh and has lived, studied, and worked across Bangladesh, Saudi Arabia, New Zealand, and Australia. His journey through diverse cultural and religious landscapes has profoundly shaped his worldview and deepened his appreciation for the rich tapestry of human belief and practice.

He approaches religious differences with a spirit of openness and empathy, firmly believing in the importance of coexistence and harmonious community life. Driven by a deep curiosity, he actively engages in conversations with Muslims and non-Muslims, seeking to understand how others perceive Islam, worship, and the many questions, debates, and contradictions around faith and practice. He values these discussions not as points of division, but as opportunities for shared reflection and learning.

About Author

A medical practitioner by profession, Dr. Shahriyar Wahab is active in his field and continues to balance his professional responsibilities with his passion for learning and sharing ideas. He is especially drawn to exploring interpretations and insights, particularly those that challenge assumptions or invite deeper understanding. He is committed to fostering awareness and thoughtful engagement with knowledge that serves a broader human purpose. Through his writing and dialogue, he aims to offer readers meaningful, reflective perspectives rooted in a sincere pursuit of truth.

www.ingramcontent.com/pod-product-compliance
Lightning Source LLC
Chambersburg PA
CBHW031149020426
42333CB00013B/585